Sam Simpson: Architect of Hope

Carol S. Garrett

New Hope
Birmingham, Alabama

Title: Sam Simpson: Architect of Hope

Dewey Decimal Classification: 266.092

Subject Headings: SIMPSON, SAMUEL G.
                  MISSIONS, HOME
                  MISSIONS—NEW YORK

ISBN: 0-936625-63-5

N894104 • 10M • 0589

Dedication

**To my parents
for a lifetime of total
love and support**

Foreword

Who Is Sam Simpson?

One of the first big-name, successful pastors I met when I became executive director of Woman's Missionary Union was Sam Simpson. We were in a retreat setting, some distance from the noise and stress of New York City. We were talking about growing churches. Many well-known specialists in church growth were present, and we were dealing with heavy matters.

I remember Sam Simpson. He has a quick wit that adds sparkle to any occasion. I remember particularly our discussion on women's roles, when I flippantly said, "I'm safe. No man wants to be executive director of WMU, SBC." To that Sam responded, "Oh, but I do, Carolyn!" His beautifully accented words earned him a fun title that day. Even more sharply he spoke to the subject at hand. I recognized that Sam Simpson knows what it means to grow churches, and that he knows that that is important.

I remember Sam Simpson. I visited him on his own turf. Silhouetted against the skyscrapers he stood, waving his arms in a wide arc, defining his church field. I walked through the hallways at the church where he shepherds a large and diverse flock. I watched the response that his presence calls forth from the staff who serve him and serve with him. I sensed that I was in the presence of a true pastor. This feeling continued as we walked through the streets with people greeting him, appearing to want to walk close to him, touch him.

I remember Sam Simpson. I remember the skill and care with which he served as president of the Baptist Convention of New York. I remember conferences where he has spoken. I recognize him as a statesman among Southern Baptists.

I remember Sam Simpson. He is friend. He is missionary. He is pastor. He is statesman. He is God's chosen servant in home missions. He is the subject of this book. Please meet Sam Simpson.

Carolyn Weatherford
Executive Director,
Woman's Missionary Union, SBC, 1974-1989

Acknowledgements

Writing this book took a great deal of effort on the part of many people. Those who helped me will never know how deeply grateful I am for their sacrifices of time and love. My sincerest thanks go to:

Sam Simpson, whose greatest desire is that God be glorified through every part of his life. I am thankful for the way he is being used by God, and for his willingness to share that story.

Lola Simpson, who gave me such personal insights into her husband, her family, and herself.

The people of Bronx Baptist Church and Wake-Eden Community Baptist Church, for the part they play in accomplishing Sam's dream of bringing their city to Christ.

The people of my church, Clearview Baptist, for their interest, encouragement, and prayers.

My Thursday night women's Bible study group, for their support at the very beginning of this project. And to Debbie Waid, who prayed for me every day while I was in New York.

Andy Wood, for being more than my pastor by also being my friend. I'll never forget his help in the times of my computer crises.

Nick Grassel, the computer wizard at Dewberry's who saved my life not once, but two times. He is a "knight in shining armor."

Cathy Butler, Janell Young, and Kathryne Solomon at Woman's Missionary Union, for their work in putting together the finished product.

Mary Poole and Audra Bean, the best back-up babysitters in the world.

Robin Wood, for being my faithful prayer partner and encourager. She believed in me even on the days when I didn't. I thank God for sending me a friend like Robin!

Nanny, into whose able and loving hands I placed my son Jake on the many days it took me to write this book. I could never have done the work without having the peace of mind that came from knowing she was taking care of my son. She is a very special mother-in-law.

My mother and daddy, for being here, just as they always are, to help me in any and every way they could. They are the definition of unconditional love.

Danny, for being my rock. His support, patience, and love throughout the many months it took to write this book were unequaled. As in every other part of my life, he was my partner and my very best friend.

Jake, my greatest inspiration.

Chapter 1

Near New York City's Bronx Baptist Church a police siren blared, but few worshipers seemed to notice. They were too busy singing, many of them with their eyes closed, swaying to the rhythm of the music. Neither boredom nor ritual had a place in the way the people sang tonight. There was a feeling of fresh experience pouring into familiar words, and the emotion appeared real, almost new. The people were worshiping, and God was in the room.

"Because he lives, I can face tomorrow; Because he lives all fear is gone; Because I know he holds the future, And life is worth the living just because he lives," the hymn rang out.[1]

Sam Simpson looked out across the faces of his congregation and thought about the significance of what ho was hearing.

For the people of his church, simple geography gave a certain amount of depth to the words of that emotional hymn. Just outside the walls of their building existed a city famous for its lack of soul or conscience, a city that could not care less about a living Jesus. Some of those singing about how fear was gone had walked past a group of tough young drug dealers just a couple of blocks from

1

the church. One man sang about the future with tears in his eyes. His only possessions were the dirty clothes on his back, his only home the streets. Yesterday he came to the church looking for a free meal, and had found salvation. Living on the front lines in a city that often resembles a battleground, these people stood singing with conviction about the worth just knowing Jesus gave to their lives.

Few of the church members were poor, hungry, or homeless, but they couldn't escape the harsh realities of their surroundings. Although most of them had good jobs, plenty to eat, and families to love, they had no buffer from the people they passed on the street, sat beside on the subway, or heard crying through thin apartment walls. Bronx Baptists couldn't dismiss New York City as an overwhelming (approximately) 7.3 million collective people too hardened or hopeless for Jesus to change. Life forced them to see New York one needy person at a time.

"Ladies and gentlemen," Sam began, "one day I'm going to walk down the streets of Heaven. And the Lord's going to take me by the arm and lead me to a special neighborhood. We're going to walk down Glory Boulevard, turn up Grace Street, and then take a stroll on Joy Avenue.

"And the Lord's going to say, 'Sam, I'm so proud of you. All these little streets have houses with people in them because of you.' I say there's enough room up on those streets for everybody in the Bronx to have their own mansion!"

The singing had long since stopped, along with the siren, and Sam neared the end of his sermon. He was painting a vivid picture of a new Bronx in Heaven. The people were with him, punctuating much of his story with loud amens.

Sam was on one of his favorite themes—building. Build-

2

ing mansions in Heaven, building relationships with people, building new apartment houses inside the burned-out shells of old ones, building ministries wherever he saw a need, building with whatever tools were available—everywhere Sam Simpson went and everything he did somehow related back to that one word. *Building.*

But even the adrenaline rush he felt from preaching on a subject so close to his heart couldn't overcome one fact tonight. Sam was tired. He didn't look or sound tired as he laughed and talked his way through the afterchurch crowd milling about in the sanctuary. Few of those talking to him would have guessed that his feet hurt or his black checkered tie was beginning to choke him. It had been a long day, and was still a long way from being over.

Sam looked around for Lola. He needed to ask her something. Finally, he saw her standing by the piano, talking to Mrs. Clemmons. Making his way to them, he could hear them discussing an upcoming local election. His usually reserved and somewhat quiet wife was energetically defending a controversial candidate's record of service to the poor.

Even after 25 years of marriage, and with many other things on his mind, Sam looked at his wife and for a moment thought about what a truly beautiful woman she was. But that wasn't what he said.

"Lols, you're much too radical to be the wife of a pastor," he teased, interrupting the discussion.

"Excuse me, Pastor," she countered with mock reverence.

"Reverend, I enjoyed your sermon, but I wish you could find a way to get to Bronx Baptist a little earlier on Sunday mornings," Mrs. Clemmons said. He had heard this complaint from her before. A Southern Baptist home missionary, Sam led Bronx Baptist to start Wake-Eden Community Baptist Church in 1972 in another part of the

3

borough. Because he was uniquely suited to meet the needs of both congregations, he pastored both.

Pastoring two churches seven miles apart makes scheduling complicated and often a bit tricky.

Because he preaches in both churches every week, some changes were made in the traditional Baptist Sunday schedule. There is no way for Sam to be in both places at 11:00 A.M. on Sunday mornings. The answer was for Wake-Eden to start its worship service at 9:00 A.M. and hold Sunday School afterward. As soon as the Wake-Eden service ends, Sam hurries to Bronx Baptist, where the deacons have already started the service if he is late.

Sam knows that as his ministry grows, the day will likely come when one or both of the churches will have a new pastor. But the Bronx is not overrun with Southern Baptist preachers. And besides that, Sam feels led to stay with both churches. He particularly likes the way the current arrangement encourages members to take on real leadership in operating the churches. In his opinion, the benefits far outweigh the problems.

Still, a few don't see things as he does. But Sam quietly works in the background and turns problems into non-problems by diffusing them. Of course, this system occasionally fails, and instead of putting out a fire, causes it to smolder. Sam knew that tonight he was looking into the face of a smoldering fire.

Mrs. Clemmons stood with her lips pursed, waiting to hear the pastor's excuse this time.

"Well, let's just say it was one of those mornings when the traffic was not on the Lord's side," he joked, seeming to take her comment lightly. If she only knew what kind of a day I've really had, he thought, she would be surprised to see me here at all.

It had been a long time since 5:30 that morning. Sam had asked God to wake him so he could fulfill his com-

4

mitment to pray for Bronx Baptist's upcoming revival. He had told his congregation God would wake them if He knew they meant business.

"And if you don't mean business with God, you'll go ahead and sleep till 7:00, because every time He shakes you the Devil will say, 'Oh, go ahead and sleep.' "

Sam believed what he had said. At 5:30 A.M. he climbed out of bed, pulled on a pair of red sweatpants, and walked into the living room where a well-worn family altar stood in front of the windows. Yawning as he tried to shake off the short night's sleep, Sam knelt and began the business of praying for revival among the people in his churches.

He has long been a believer that there is no way to keep the momentum of his life going without what he calls "really being in touch." When he asked his congregations to commit to extra prayertime for the upcoming revival, he reminded them of Jesus' habit of spending all night in prayer before some big event in His life. He told them again and again that to be productive, their prayer life must be intact. And he drilled home the idea that whether a person's prayertime lasted 15 minutes or 2 hours, the important factors were the condition of the heart and a right relationship with the Father.

Sam realizes it is hard for people to actually live such biblical principles, especially in a world that constantly pulls them in other directions. He knows how difficult it is to make time in his own busy life for prayer. He isn't always successful at keeping in constant communication with God. But he loves the idea of what that constant, intimate contact can do in a person's life. Today as he thought about revival in his churches, he prayed that they would all move a little closer to such a life-style.

Stretching as he got up from the altar, Sam wound his way down three narrow sets of stairs to the basement.

Here he would really begin meeting the schedule of his busiest day of the week.

A big, brightly lit room, the basement is piled high with almost 20 years of Sam Simpson's personal history. Files and records, the children's discarded belongings, equipment being stored for the churches, box after box of slides and photographs, furniture waiting to be reupholstered, all sorts of unidentifiable stuff occupy almost every square inch of space. And everything in this giant maze is dropped neatly into its own little stack. Sam's basement is like his own private world.

A small exercise bicycle is wedged between a portable dividing wall and a folding table filled with piles of papers that are to one day become a book Sam is planning to write. Humming a nameless tune, he got on the bike and rode his allotted 15 minutes.

Ready for his usual time of devotion and meditation, Sam went further back into the basement to his study, the little room that is about as far away from the rest of the world as he can get.

Like the rest of the basement, the study is crammed with many stacks of books, papers, letters, and various other ordinary things common to a preacher. But there are also pictures of Sam with Jimmy Carter, Pierre Trudeau, Desmond Tutu. There are certificates of appreciation for service as president or executive director of several different Southern Baptist and other groups, as well as letters of thanks from local and state political leaders. Awards citing him as an outstanding black American and as an outstanding Jamaican hang on the walls,

Here in this little cubbyhole office Sam executes many duties, including those of leading the entire Southern Baptist body of New York as its state convention president.

Evidence of his achievements decorate Sam's office, but not his personality. Like most successful people, he has a healthy ego. A very strong personality, it is his nature to be confident. He trusts his instincts, pushes hard to get what he wants, and seldom acknowledges obstacles to his plans.

But his ego takes a backseat to his desire to relate to people. Sam Simpson is the kind of man New Yorkers can meet, talk to, and never know that he is more than just "pastor." Although holding a place of prominence in his profession and his community, Sam always remembers that he is first a missionary and a pastor. And most of all, he never forgets that he is just a man, struggling with life like everybody else.

Sitting down behind his desk, Sam put on his glasses and opened his Bible. Some mornings he just sits there and reflects, thinking about things he has learned in past prayertimes. It seems the more he studies and prays, the more he realizes how difficult "walking the Christian pathway" really is in his world. He also becomes more and more aware of his own human weaknesses and frailties when it comes to carrying out some of the things he feels God demands.

Today he did some last-minute preparation on his sermons. He would be preaching on revival to both churches, but the two messages would be slightly different. Sam had been working for a while when Lola buzzed him. They had installed a special telephone line to keep her from making the long trek downstairs every time she needed to talk to him. Breakfast was ready, and one of the deacons was on the other line to ask him something about Bronx Baptist's photocopy machine.

Sam talked to the deacon for several minutes, told him where to find the key to the machine in his desk at the church, and then hurried upstairs before the eggs were completely cold.

He entered the kitchen to find Lola and Kim his teen-

7

aged daughter getting ready for church. They were a study in contrasts. Lola stood at the sink, sedately scrubbing a skillet. Moving at her own pace, she didn't seem concerned about how much time was left to finish getting ready for church. Kim was running around with a piece of toast in one hand and a wrinkled dress in the other, looking all over the house for the iron. Even in the old fleecy bathrobe, she looked more like a model for a teenage magazine than a preacher's daughter.

"Good morning, Kimmy," Sam said, snatching a peck on the cheek as she raced by. The thing that amazed him was that for all of Lola's apparent disregard for time, she was almost never late, and Kim was the one who would dash in at the last minute.

"Where is Stephen?" Sam asked.

"He has decided not to join us this morning," Lola said matter-of-factly.

Sam sighed, a thing he seldom did. At times his older daughter Erica had tested him as she grew up. Stephen did the same thing, and he knew so would Kim. His philosophy about children allowed him to give his best advice, guidance, and support, and then be free of guilt if they made mistakes by choosing not to do as he said. That philosophy sounded good and usually worked. But children have a way of turning most philosophies, at some time or other, inside out.

It was time to start thinking about the day ahead. After a hurried breakfast, Sam showered and dressed quickly. Straightening his tie in the bathroom mirror, he called back to Lola that he would see her at church. Gathering up his briefcase, Bible, and a few loose papers, he went outside to walk the few blocks to Wake-Eden. He would rather have taken his car, but he had not seen it since he left the keys in it one morning a few months ago.

That day he had been hurrying to meet an appointment,

and realized he didn't have his briefcase as he backed out of the driveway. He honked the horn so Lola would come to the door. Then he jumped out of the car without even turning off the ignition and ran up the stairs for the briefcase. She handed it to him before he came inside the house, and he turned around to see a strange woman driving off in his brand-new vehicle. He dropped the briefcase and ran down the steps to the sidewalk, but she was long gone.

That happened several months ago, and Sam was tired of haggling with the insurance company over the money to replace it. In the meantime, transportation had become a sort of game to him. Every day he faced a busy schedule that demanded he find someone to either drive him around or loan him a car. Seldom did he think about how he was going to get somewhere before it was time to go. But somehow Sam always seemed to run into a friend with a car or be talking to someone on the phone who could take him. Sundays were particularly challenging.

This morning he had just started down the sidewalk when he heard a car slow down behind him and honk its horn. Sam smiled to himself and turned around. There was one of his deacons on his way to church. Did the pastor want a ride? He got in, and by the time they stopped for Sam to get out at Wake-Eden's front door, he had arranged to borrow the car to get to Bronx Baptist.

As Sam ran up the church steps, he saw a group of nervous looking college students standing close to the door. The summer missionaries! He had temporarily forgotten they were here, even though he had given them his official greeting when they arrived yesterday. Fresh off the airplane from places like Sandy Hook, Mississippi, and Waco, Texas, eight of them had come to spend ten weeks working at Wake-Eden and Bronx Baptist. Now that they had arrived, they weren't quite sure why they

9

were here or what to do with themselves.

Straight from the heart of the Bible Belt, they were eager to see the worst New York had to offer and claim it for Christ. After experiencing the city for less than 24 hours, most of them were a little perplexed at what they had seen—or maybe at what they had not seen.

One boy couldn't believe there were actually trees and houses in the Bronx. He hadn't expected to see anything but skyscrapers and asphalt the whole time he was here. Others wanted to know where the graffiti-covered buildings were, the garbage on the streets, the bumper-to-bumper traffic, the rude and unsmiling people. One of the girls was terrified, expecting to be mugged in broad daylight, while another couldn't wait to see a real street gang.

They were all looking for their stereotypes and many of them seemed disappointed about not finding them. It was almost as if they would have been more comfortable in the New York they had imagined. The city they found was not nearly as exotic and in many ways seemed a lot like home. This discovery would force a big change in their perceptions of just what they were supposed to do this summer.

They looked at Sam with relief, hoping he would give them some much desired direction. Instead, he greeted them all with warmth and enthusiasm as he glanced down at his watch, realizing the time. There were many questions which Sam really could not answer for them right then. He quickly told them that they would be introduced in the Wake-Eden service, be asked to say a few words of testimony, and after church go to Bronx Baptist to do the same thing again.

Not yet accustomed to Sam's light Jamaican accent, they strained to understand what he was telling them. Nobody was sure exactly what they were to do. They didn't quite know what to make of Sam, especially his sense of humor.

In their eagerness to please him and appear willing to do whatever he asked, they took every word he said seriously. Because they were out of their element, they just didn't realize that Sam had been joking about much of what he had told them the night before.

Would they really have to walk to Bronx Baptist Church? And would the services really last four or five hours? One of the boys held a brown paper bag full of peanut butter and jelly sandwiches for the group because Sam had said they would probably have to eat during the church services.

He knew the missionaries were uneasy. They always were at first. Every summer different students come to work with his churches. They are a great help, but almost never in the ways they imagine they will be. He looks forward to seeing them gel as a group and develop their own sense of ministry and purpose.

As he went inside the church, Sam asked one of the men to get the Wake-Eden van and take the missionaries to Bronx Baptist after the service.

People were milling about in the foyer outside the sanctuary, beginning to make their way inside before church started. In many ways this church in the heart of the Bronx, New York, is typically Southern Baptist. A Cooperative Program poster hangs on one wall, and an Annie Armstrong Easter Offering poster on another, next to a WMU bulletin board. The same Sunday School books and offering envelopes that are being used all over the Southern Baptist Convention are stacked on a table in the corner.

The demographics of most of the membership would classify them as typical American families. Mothers and fathers work, usually in professional positions, to bring home an average joint income of $50,000 to $60,000. In expensive New York City, that amount of money has to

11

be stretched so that they can save in hopes of buying a house and sending their children to college.

Most of the people living in the Bronx are black or Hispanic. The membership of both Bronx and Wake-Eden is mainly black Jamaican. Sam knows that it is common in the city for ethnic groups to come together to form their own neighborhoods and churches. He is Jamaican himself. But he is determined that his churches be based on more than just common ethnic heritage. He believes they should reach out to their entire community, crossing barriers of any kind. In this way a church can ensure that it will not only survive, but thrive.

For all they have done to assimilate themselves into the Southern Baptist mainstream, when the worship service starts it is clear that Wake-Eden Community Baptist Church proudly retains a rich Jamaican tradition. The dignity and ceremony of the service reflects the English influence on their heritage.

The choir, deacons, and pastor enter from the rear of the church and proceed down the center aisle. The hymns and choir specials are more often stately anthems than the gospel music usually associated with black worship services. There is warmth and spontaneity, but everything is done with order and decorum.

When Sam preaches, his style combines that of Jamaican, American black, and Southern Baptist. To get his point across, he can be as intellectual as the most highly educated Jamaican, as soulful as the most passionate American black, or as traditional as the most typical Southern Baptist. Today he had chosen the good Samaritan, enjoying the opportunity to tell a familiar Bible story in a Bronx setting.

"Do you remember the time a gentleman came to Jesus and asked him, 'Who is my neighbor?'

"And Jesus said to him, 'Oh fella, listen to me. A guy

went all the way from Bronx to Manhattan. And when he got to the Willis Avenue Bridge, there was a gang down under the bridge. They pulled him down and cut him, and did all kinds of terrible things to him.'

"And Jesus said there was a Roman Catholic priest who passed by and he saw the guy down there and he looked at him and said, 'I'm on my way to church.'

"And then the Presbyterian came by, well decked with his collar and robe, and he looked and saw the man and he said, 'I wish I had the time.'

"And the good old Baptist minister came by, possibly Sam Simpson, and he looked at that man and said, 'Oh boy, I'm late. I'm rushing to Bronx Baptist Church to preach. If I'm not there this morning, nothing will take place.' And then he looked down at the man and said, 'I wish I could say Get up man and rise, but I can't because my faith is weak. It is strong in Jesus, but it is weak in telling you to get up, and so I might as well run on to church.'

"So we all left that man there. Then a little guy came by who was not as religious as we are, but who lived in communication with God. And he was not too busy for this man. So he reached down and said, 'In spite of what may happen to me, I am going to embrace you.' And he took him up.''

Jesus used this illustration, Sam said, to tell us to do what is available to be done.

"In the midst of drugs, crime, sexual sin, pollution, and so many other bad things, how can we be silent? How can we not make ourselves available?'' Sam had challenged the congregation.

At the end of the service, three people were presented who had come forward for salvation several weeks earlier. After counseling, they had later been baptized. Today they were being voted into the church. Sam embraced each one, gave each a word of encouragement, and then assigned a Scripture portion for each to memorize. He chose Scripture verses to fit each person's particular need. To the man who had all his life been characterized as slow and unable to learn, Sam gave John 3:16. There was no need for anyone to be left out of God's victories.

By now it was almost 10:30 and Bronx Baptist Church was waiting. The deacon who had promised Sam his car was parked at the curb right in front of the church. He handed Sam the keys.

"Thank you, my good friend!" Sam said heartily as he opened the door. Everyone is his "good friend." Those words trip off of his tongue with a Jamaican lilt, but they are more than just an expression to him.

Sam learned early in life that the more people you know, the easier it is to get things done. The world has given a name to this kind of relationship building. It is called networking. In a system that encourages survival of the fittest, many people use networking to come out on top. But for Sam it is a way to beat the system and allow the underdog to also come out on top.

In Sam's network, a friend is anyone with whom he comes in contact. This attitude is a natural part of his personality, a fortunate thing for him. Establishing relationships with all kinds of people from all walks of life is essential when ministering in a city the size of New York. Networking is the key to making any real changes. Sam has been networking for so long he does it constantly now, almost without thinking.

He has to build networks because his business is rebuilding lives. And to Sam Simpson, rebuilding a life means renewing human dignity as well as rescuing a soul. Poverty, crime, hunger, and homelessness are more than sin to Sam. They are symptoms. He cannot minister to the spiritual needs of his community without reacting to

14

the massive, overwhelming social needs.

Some have called the Bronx the most famous slum in America. Sam knows both the realities and the exaggerations of that reputation. But he doesn't get a view of his missions field just from the evening news. He goes out into the community and listens to the people. He looks at the children. He experiences their pain. And he looks around for some stepping stone these people can use to begin their climb out of misery.

When Sam sees a hungry man on the street, he wants him to have a place where he can find food. When he sees lonely people staring out of dirty apartment windows, he wants to find some way to show them that life hasn't passed them by. When he sees children growing up surrounded by crime and violence, he wants to make a place where they can go and feel love.

When he looks at row after row of burned-out, useless apartment buildings, he sees the empty and burned-out lives they represent. As Sam wants to rebuild those burned-out buildings, he wants to rebuild the lives. And when he sees a problem that is bigger than he or his churches can handle alone, he looks around for someone who will join them in the fight.

Sam knows that New York is a big city. But he also knows he serves a big God. That is why he can lie down at night after a grueling Sunday and be excited about Monday. He knows that God will be doing something exciting in the Bronx on Monday, and he wants to be in on it.

Chapter 2

"Good morning, Pastor!" the roomful of noisy preschoolers shouted in singsong cadence as Sam entered the door of Wake-Eden Christian Academy.

What a way to start a Monday! Facing the loud enthusiasm of that many children so early in the morning might have sent some of his fellow New Yorkers running back underground to the subway. But Sam found it music to his ears.

A few of the children crowded around him as he came through the door. Class hadn't started yet, and the big cheerful room was full of boys and girls from the surrounding community.

They were excited about seeing each other, seeing the pastor, and seeing their teachers. They were excited about the day ahead, and its promised field trip to the zoo. They were excited because they had lost a tooth, or because they were wearing new shoes, or because they had seen a policeman's horse on the way to school.

In general, they were just excited about being alive, and this energy spilled out of them and all over anyone who came into their ready-to-start-the-day world. Sam likes to come by and soak up a little of that excitement.

To him the schools, more than anything, are tangible

evidence of how his churches reach out to minister in their communities. Most of the parents living nearby work, and child care is a real need. Sam's churches are committed to meeting needs, so both Bronx Baptist and Wake-Eden find it natural to provide that care by locating schools inside the church buildings. They operate fully licensed preschools year-round, in addition to an afterschool program for school-age children. In the summer they add day camps and Vacation Bible School to the agenda.

Sam usually spends his Tuesdays working at Wake-Eden, but he had come by today to pick up a few papers and make some calls. Sometimes he just liked to drop in early and visit with the children.

"Pastor, Pastor, hello."

He sat five-year-old Tanya down and thanked her for the crayon portrait of himself, then turned to speak to Maisie Bruce, the school's director.

"Brucie, my goodly lady, how are you this fine morning?" he asked.

Sam's Jamaican accent seems to become more pronounced when he talks to Maisie Bruce. She too is a Southern Baptist home missionary who came to New York from Jamaica. Her accent is still strong, as are the ties to her homeland, where she visits several times a year. While her roots remain in Jamaica, her heart is firmly planted in Wake-Eden Christian Academy.

She and Sam usually talk a little politics or exchange some bit of news about friends before dealing with business. But today Maisie Bruce had programs for the upcoming children's musical on her mind.

The preschoolers' energy was not revitalizing her at the moment, and she motioned for the teachers to start classes. She and Sam walked out to a little area that served as the entry hall for the school. They sat down on a wooden bench to discuss the programs for the musical. Sam volunteered Lola to do the typing.

He looked past Maisie into the classroom and saw that the teachers had quieted the children enough to separate into age groups. Hardwood floors creaked as little chairs were pulled out from under little tables and children sat down to begin their first activity.

Portable walls divided the room. Brightly colored letters of the alphabet made from construction paper fluttered overhead in the breeze of the air conditioner. A giant Sesame Street mural, painted by a past group of summer missionaries, covered the back wall. Various posters and pictures decorated the other walls. Some were of animals and birds. Some were of children helping their parents, and some conveyed biblical themes. There was a picture of Martin Luther King, Jr.; a poster from the health department with a reminder about immunizations; and artwork made by the children.

"Everything about that room says, This is a happy place," Sam thought.

But at least one person in the room wasn't happy. She was sitting at a table with the younger children, her back to the door. Amy, a summer missionary from Oklahoma, had been completely overwhelmed by the reception the kids had given her.

She was as strange to them as they were to her. Her long blonde hair and fair complexion fascinated the black and Hispanic children. Sam had warned the summer missionaries that the children would not feel inhibited by their difference in race and culture, only interested. It was important, he had told them, to deal with whatever prejudices they had before confronting a group of youngsters eager to hold their hands or touch their faces.

Amy thought she was ready, but discovered she wasn't. She had expected the children to be poor and dirty, maybe even hungry. In her mind the black and Hispanic children of New York City were victims of neglect, abuse, and an overall lack of love. Amy was prepared to be a self-sacrificing missionary to the poor and underprivileged. But the children at Wake-Eden were not as she had envisioned.

Most of them came from stable, two-parent homes. Some of the mothers who brought children to the church that morning wore nurses uniforms. Amy's own mother was a nurse. They hugged and kissed their children as they said good-bye. None of them looked dirty or hungry and most appeared to be wearing new clothes.

Sam had warned the missionaries to deal with their feelings because he knows how deceptive prejudice can be. Not one of them believed themselves to be prejudiced. But he knew from experience that they would all discover feelings that would surprise and bother them. Dealing with those feelings would help them grow and mature.

Amy, serious about her commitment to sharing Christ this summer, was experiencing her first confrontation with her own hidden prejudices, and found it very unsettling. She was sincerely ready and willing to minister to people of a different race. But she hadn't realized until this morning that she was prepared to do so only when they fit into her preconceived mold. The children around her came from families much like her own. She had expected them to be so different. How could they be so much the same?

Every year Sam sees young summer missionaries grapple with feelings such as Amy's. He stays in the background as much as possible, allowing them to work things out on their own. By the end of summer, they will have changed more dramatically than they realize. The discovery of their prejudices will be put into perspective by a far more enlightening realization.

What Sam wants these summer missionaries—and every

group of volunteers who come to the Bronx—to see is the great need for love. While it is true that many people in the Bronx are desperately poor, many are not. Many live day in and day out with nobody in the world to care about them. But others live surrounded by a large, warm circle of family and friends.

The great sad truth is that no matter what the circumstances, most of the people in the Bronx live without the love of Christ. This is the love Sam wants the volunteers to share, and so he watches with interest as they discover new things about themselves.

Right now, as he talked to Maisie, Sam could see that Amy was in trouble. One of the teachers had gone to the supply room for more crayons and had asked Amy to begin the lesson on sharing. Sensing an easy mark, the kids quickly took over the situation, and Amy could not regain control.

The teacher returned to find her sitting in the floor literally covered in children, yelling at them to get back in their seats. Sam saw the entire episode, but decided to let Amy handle it herself. He had an idea how she was feeling.

"What a way to start a Monday," she thought, disappointed at her beginning. This was definitely not the way she had imagined her first day as a summer missionary. She didn't believe she'd ever be able to make any meaningful impact on these kids. She had lost confidence in her ability to relate to them, especially about anything spiritual.

All they wanted to talk about was their impending trip to the zoo. Amy felt terrified at the prospect of herding this group into a subway. But the teachers assured her they did it many times every summer, and she would be taking them by herself before long.

"Fat chance of that," she thought. Only their prediction

that she would soon be driving the church van all over the Bronx seemed more remote or terrifying.

She wondered how the other summer missionaries were doing. Some were assigned to Wake-Eden and some to Bronx Baptist. At least they thought they were. They still weren't clear on their exact assignments and had pushed Sam for an orientation meeting. One night this week they were all supposed to go out to eat and talk about duties and expectations. Everybody would be glad to settle that. He had several meetings already scheduled this week, but told them they would try to work out a time.

Amy looked through the doorway and saw Sam and Maisie sitting on the bench laughing.

"If he's too busy to set a time for us, how come he can sit out there all morning and joke around?" she said to herself.

Just then Corey, one of the youngest children in the school, tapped her on the shoulder and handed her a paper flower he had made from tissue paper. He smiled tentatively at Amy as she took the gift.

"What's wrong with me?" she thought. "I've only been here three days and God is already having to send little kids to remind me where my heart is supposed to be."

She sat Corey in her lap and turned to look out the door again. Sam was gone. "Thanks for the attitude adjustment, God," she prayed quickly.

Sam had told them not to judge people or situations too quickly in the Bronx. She had no idea he was aware of the problems she and the other missionaries faced. He just ministered to different people in different ways, and ministering to them right now meant letting them find some things out for themselves.

She also couldn't have known that slowing down to share a laugh is one of Sam's best secret weapons for ministry. Talking with Maisie Bruce, he realized how tired she was and how heavily the upcoming musical was weighing on her.

She knew that the children's musical was one of her few chances to present the gospel directly to all the parents at one time. Many of them did not attend church, but they would come to see their children perform. While she wanted the music to be good and the children to have fun, she really desired to reach those parents. The responsibility of that task, coupled with preparing the children and handling all the production details, was exhausting her.

Sam thought she needed a good laugh to help retain her perspective. He hoped he would never become too busy to have time for a little fun, especially when a friend needed a boost.

"I must remember to make a note to call Lola, after I call Ted, and see when she can type those programs," he said to himself as he walked outside. He wanted to see if the church van was parked nearby. It wasn't, but he was glad he had stepped outdoors.

An unusual cool spell put a springlike chill in the summer air. A light breeze drifted down from a cloudless blue sky and rustled the leaves of trees lining the sidewalk.

"What a great day to be alive!" Sam thought as he stopped to enjoy the beautiful New York morning. The sky was not the blue of a Jamaican sky, and the breeze lacked the taste of salt from the ocean, but that didn't matter to him. God had brought him a long way from idyllic Jamaican vistas, but had given him a vision of the unique beauty of the city.

"Such a God," Sam thought, "to put me in a place like the Bronx and make it home in my heart."

Suddenly the strains of "Jesus Loves Me" escaped from behind the closed classroom windows. The children sang so loudly that they could be heard outside above the noise of the street.

Sam folded his arms and put a finger across his lips as he stood there listening. The words were muffled, but understandable. He could picture the trusting little faces turned up to the teachers, singing songs about Jesus.

"How far we've come," he thought.

In some ways it was hard to remember that cold January morning in 1976 when they opened the doors of the day school for the first time. But somehow it seemed like yesterday.

Wake-Eden was still a chapel then. There was no money to speak of, and no real books or supplies. All they had was a desire to reach out into the community and meet a growing need. Maisie Bruce, a certified social worker, school administrator, and member of Wake-Eden agreed to head the day-school project.

That first morning three little students arrived at nine o'clock. They refused to take off their coats and hats and clung tearfully to their mothers. The room wasn't colorful or happy at all. It was drab and a little cold. There weren't lots of classmates to ease the fear of being left alone. They had only each other, and their mothers were about to leave. Never mind that by one o'clock they would be happily back at home, and two other children would have come to take their places in the afternoon session.

It had been a hard beginning for everyone. The mothers struggled to leave, the children struggled against being left, and the teachers struggled to make everyone happy. They wanted this school to work.

Day after day little hands were pulled from their mothers' and placed in the teachers', who tried hard to overcome the childrens' fears with love and patience. As teachers worked with the children those first few days, their minds raced with ways to improve their plans. By the end of the week they were certain the cold weather and blank walls had been major contributors to the prevalent unhappy attitudes.

23

Those early problems began to be solved. Lesson plans and programs took shape. Slowly the children began learning new songs and stories which they shared with their parents when they went home.

Lola joined two other women who began serving as substitute volunteer teachers, and she enrolled their younger daughter Kim in the school. They would come home with stories, good and bad, about the day's events. Sam could tell that the day school was succeeding just by listening to them.

But even with all the optimism, a cold New York winter did its best to stamp out the efforts of the school. Some days were so bad the children refused to come. Everyone looked forward to spring.

By Easter the teachers and a few parents took the children on their first field trip. It was hard to tell who was more excited, the adults or the students, as they walked into Radio City Music Hall to see the Easter show.

More new students came, and a parent-teacher association formed. The association changed the name of the school from Community Baptist Chapel Nursery School to Wake-Eden Christian Academy. By June there were 11 students enrolled. Four of them graduated that month with great ceremony.

"And now 81 children come to school here, with people clamoring to be placed on the waiting list," Sam thought.

Beep! Beep!

A silver van pulled over to the curb next to Sam. Ted Jefferson leaned out the window and grinned.

"Sam, don't you have anything better to do than stand on the sidewalk daydreaming?"

"Well you see, Mr. Jefferson, I knew that if I stood here long enough I was certain to see you out cruising around in this expensive vehicle, and it would save me the trouble of making a phone call," Sam replied. "By the way, who's running the office?''

''I'm doing all the work from the van now. We're changing the name to Mobile Shepherds Restoration Corporation,'' Ted said.

On and on they went, sticking each other with good-natured barbs. Sam and Ted had been friends for a long time, and now that Ted had been named executive director of the Shepherds Restoration Corporation they worked together too.

The Shepherds, as the group is more commonly known, is an organization made up of more than 80 churches. They banded together in the 1970s to combat some of the severe social problems then confronting the Bronx. Their main concern was providing housing. Sam had been instrumental in organizing the group, and now served as president.

''I need to talk to you about this grant we're asking the borough president for. Why don't you come by for lunch so we can go over the application form? I'm on my way to work on it right now,'' Sam said.

The only thing Sam really doesn't like about his job is the paperwork. The problem is, to get anything done in a city the size of New York, there is always some form to complete or letter to write. He usually waits until the last possible minute to deal with paperwork.

''OK, Sam. I'll stop by the office and get my file on that grant. You want me to pick you up around noon?''

''Why don't we say a quarter till? What do you feel like eating? Chinese?'' he asked.

''Where?''

''How about Hawaii Moon?''

The food there tasted authentic, and Sam needed to speak to the owner about purchasing an ad for Wake-Eden's anniversary banquet program. He figured he could kill several birds with one stone.

"Aren't they pretty crowded that time of day?" Ted asked, thinking of some afternoon appointments.

"Well, yes, but the head waiter and I have this understanding," Sam said.

"I should have known. Does the FBI know about your system of contacts, Pastor?" Ted laughed.

Sam just closed his eyes and smiled.

"Oh, by the way, Ted, after lunch could you possibly . . . ?"

"Yes, Sam, I'll take you to Bronx Baptist. I'd better get out of here before I have to cancel my afternoon meetings!"

Ted waved out the window as he drove away.

Sam went inside the church to find the form he needed to complete for Ted. He forgot about calling Lola to ask her when she could type the program for the musical.

Several messages waited in his office. Call for reservations about the New York City Council of Churches luncheon this week. Call Bronx Baptist Church. The Jamaican Counsel General had returned his call. Call the Baptist state office to set up a conference call with three other state convention presidents. Another message to call Bronx Baptist. It wasn't yet eleven o'clock, and he wasn't even supposed to be here today.

Sam did not have a secretary, so several people had answered his phone. He shuffled through the messages again, hoping to see one from the insurance company about his car. That was the one call he had been expecting after a heated conversation with them on Friday. No message.

"That figures," Sam thought as he sat down and began looking for the grant application he'd been discussing with Ted. Like his study at home, this office was filled with stack after stack of everything under the sun. Sam had created the filing system, and only he could decipher it.

He found the form immediately, in a folder marked Shepherds Grant, right under a stack of last Sunday's bulletins, which were sitting on top of a case of candy the youth group was going to sell.

"Let's see. Name of organization requesting grant."

The telephone rang. Sister Hagues was still at Bronx Baptist and needed to talk to him. She was in charge of the singles retreat this weekend, and wanted to know about transportation. Sam reminded her which committee chairman was in charge of those questions and quickly got off the phone.

"Delegation is the key," he chuckled under his breath as he once again turned to the form. The telephone rang again.

"Divine intervention!" Sam said out loud as he picked up the receiver. It was Ray Boggs calling from Colorado. He and his wife, Frances, had spent about four years as volunteers working with Sam in the Bronx. Now they came back to visit whenever they could. He was calling today to talk about when they might come.

"Ray, my friend! I'm delighted to hear from you. Tell me now . . ." and Sam was off. They talked for a long time, catching up on things and reminiscing a little. When they finally hung up, it was almost time for Ted to be back. There wasn't time to finish the form, so he put it in his briefcase. He would just get Ted to work on it with him.

"Delegation," he thought, turning out the light in his office.

Ted was on time and Sam was waiting at the curb. They stopped by his house to see if Lola wanted to join them for lunch, but she hadn't returned from class. She was studying nursing at a nearby college. The Hawaii Moon was crowded, but the head waiter managed to find a table. Sam and Ted talked for a long time about the presidential primaries, and over lunch had a lengthy discussion about the pros and cons of the Shepherds being politically active in the borough.

After they finally got around to finishing the work Sam brought, Ted looked at his watch and realized he was already late for his afternoon appointment.

"We gotta go, Sam," he said, hurriedly getting up and throwing his napkin on the table.

Sam told Ted not to feel bad, that all the children at Bronx Baptist preschool were waiting on him to practice their musical.

"Why do they have to wait on you to practice?" Ted asked.

"I am to be the voice of God," Sam said without thinking. That was all Ted needed, and all Sam heard about on the way to Bronx Baptist.

He went rushing in to find that the teachers and children were indeed waiting on him. The adults weren't very happy about having wasted 20 minutes trying to entertain 41 preschoolers, but Sam apologized and they all went straight upstairs to practice. Everything went smoothly, and they were finished in 30 minutes.

The teachers and Sam all knew that a good practice wouldn't necessarily bear any resemblance to the actual performance. You cannot predict what would happen when you put all those children together on a stage in front of their parents.

Every year Sam started the program with a flowery welcome to make the parents feel comfortable and at home. It worked, because every year they ignored his request not to wave at or otherwise distract the children during the performance.

If the teachers weren't careful, they would completely lose control as parents and children waved and talked back and forth in the middle of the program. It was not unusual for Sam to interrupt the program with another plea to the parents, but by that time it was too late. Most of the children recited their lines and sang their solos perfectly, but usually there was at least one stagestruck performer overcome by tears of fright at his big moment.

Marching around the stage in costumes of pajamas, bathrobes, or some other assigned attire, the children practically burst with pride. Often they held props appropriate to the song or dialogue, and these could become a hazard. One year a little girl became so excited about her giant rubber alligator during the Noah's Ark song that she started hitting other children in the head as she swung him around by the tail.

And then there is always the danger of some little ham stealing the show. One year the final song was designed to really reach adult hearts with the gospel. And it probably would have reached a few, if it hadn't had such a catchy beat.

The children were all lined across the front of the stage for the finale. The music started and they began singing at the top of their lungs. One little boy, third from the left on the front row, couldn't resist playing an imaginary guitar.

Some in the audience began to notice and started to giggle. The more they laughed, the harder he played. Before long, everyone in the room was laughing and clapping as he danced around the stage with his imaginary guitar. Few people heard the words of the song, but the little boy received a standing ovation.

"No," Sam thought as he walked back downstairs with the children and teachers, "things don't always go as we've planned."

But the parents came and took part, and left feeling proud of their children and good about the preschool.

You never knew what opportunities such contact might bring, he thought.

Just then Sam almost bumped into one of the assistant teachers who had been in the kitchen preparing the afternoon snack. He stopped to talk with her for a few minutes.

This woman's life had changed dramatically in the past year. She and her husband had lived with their two children in a shabby apartment just a few blocks away from the church. One day after a particularly violent argument he literally threw his wife and children out on the street. She had nowhere to turn, and was too afraid of her husband to go back. Thinking of Bronx Baptist Church where her children attended preschool, she went there for help. The church gave her love, understanding, and permission to stay in an apartment upstairs.

She was not a member of the church, but they treated her with kindness and respect. The love of Christ was made real to her before she even realized what was happening. The people of Bronx Baptist helped her turn the most terrifying situation of her life into a way out of her hopeless cycle of violence. She accepted Christ and was baptized. With the help of other church members, she moved into an apartment and began making a home for her children. She found it in her heart to pray for her husband.

It is a sad thing to Sam that many other victims of the violence and poverty surrounding Bronx Baptist will never find their way to the church. Unlike the Wake-Eden area, in many ways this community fits the image of an inner-city slum. Drugs are more visible, crime more common, and fear more real. Many people live in dingy apartment buildings with graffiti-covered walls. Some buildings stand empty, completely burned out on the inside. The average family income is low, and often a family has only one parent bringing that income home.

All around you can see signs of transition. On a few streets brand-new buildings stand next to burned-out and abandoned structures. Some businesses once closed are reopening. People are slowly regaining a sense of community. Bronx Baptist Church is a beacon of hope in itself.

Through the ministry of the preschool, Sam can see real changes taking place in peoples' lives. Some mothers are able to work only because the preschool is there for their children. A few parents have even started attending church through their contact with the school.

Sam stopped to watch one of the teachers help a little girl practice a prayer she was to recite in the musical.

Now before I run to play,
Let me not forget to pray
To God who kept me through the night,
And woke me with the morning light.

He was about to applaud loudly when he noticed the teacher giving further instructions.

"And ask your parents to let you practice it every morning when you get up. Be sure to say it loud enough for them to hear the words."

"You do that, sweetheart. You just never know what might happen," Sam said, smiling at the child and her teacher.

Chapter 3

It has often been said that a church takes on the personality of its pastor. If this saying is true, what is a church to do when its pastor refuses to acknowledge any limitations on obeying God's command to reach out to a needy world?

For the people of Wake-Eden and Bronx Baptist churches, having this kind of pastor means many things.

It means they will be open to any and every possibility for meeting human need. They will see the people around them more in terms of what they can be than in terms of what they are. They will be creative and innovative and ready to try new things. They will turn their focus out instead of in. They will begin to become familiar with miracles, and they will experience the joy and the power of seeing God move in places where the rest of the world believed He could never be found.

And on this particular Friday night it meant that Bronx Baptist Church was a "happening place to be." Sam loves seeing his churches busy and filled with people. Tonight he stopped outside the open basement door where the youth were having their weekly Bible study. He stood there listening for a moment.

It was Friday night in New York. The streets of this city

could satisfy every possible teenage curiosity, good and bad. The allure of glamour and excitement was there. The temptations were there, and the dangers were there. All that the world has to offer waited just outside the walls of Bronx Baptist Church.

But for some reason, for at least one Friday night, 15 young people turned their backs on that worldly standard of pleasure and excitement. Instead they decided to come to a church basement and talk about Jesus.

That in itself was miracle enough for Sam. He smiled as he turned to unlock the door to his office.

Within minutes people began to filter in and out of the room. Sam was making copies of the agenda for the seven o'clock church officers meeting. Sister Hagues arrived tired from a hard day at work but excited about the weekend singles' retreat. Five women from Bronx Baptist were going to the conference and were leaving from the church.

Officers began arriving for their meeting, and children could be heard playing in the hall. The sound of someone practicing a song on the organ drifted down from the sanctuary.

Tonight the church was a world unto itself. But as the people inside the safety of those walls focused on themselves, they were preparing to better turn their attention outward. By tomorrow the scene would change drastically.

Tomorrow the doors would open and spicy aromas would drift out from the church kitchen into the street, inviting the hungry to come inside. Members of the Woman's Missionary Union would come and put together a large home-type meal that would be offered free to the homeless people in the area. Sometimes as many as 70 or 80 would be served, sometimes fewer. The WMU never knew how many would drift in for the hot meal.

Sam often dropped by on Saturdays to eat lunch with whoever was there. He would go back into the kitchen, sampling the food as he went by, and ask how many had been there so far, who had come, what were their circumstances.

Usually the people who came by for the meal were alone. Sometimes two of them would appear to be together. And then occasionally, whole families would eat there. One week a woman brought her three children by for a meal. They lived in a nearby subway station.

The men and women who came usually sat quietly at the long metal table, looking down or staring into space as they ate. Two or three of the church members might be mingling among them, often holding a Bible and pointing out Scripture verses as they talked.

Some of the visitors smiled politely, just humoring another do-gooder in order to get a good meal. Some listened and asked questions, but merely as a pastime. Some were obviously troubled; some cried; and a few were angry. And some, like the man who came forward just last Sunday, were saved.

There wasn't anything extraordinary about the church members who came to witness to these people. They didn't have a certain technique or a polished presentation. Often they were shy and inarticulate. The only real confidence many of them had came from what they were telling.

Once they demonstrated to the people that they cared enough about them to fill their empty stomachs with food, it wasn't very hard to say, "Now I want to show you how to fill your empty life with hope."

When a person from desperate circumstances does respond to Christ, the church then shows more love by assuming the responsibility of helping them see their new commitment become reality. If a homeless man prays to accept Christ, he is counseled so there is no doubt he knows what he is doing, and why. He is then enrolled in a special enquirers' class, and it might be several weeks before he is baptized. The church helps determine that his decision is real.

The last thing Sam wants to see his churches do is offer false hope to someone who is hopeless. A meaningless prayer prayed with a lack of understanding and commitment would no more change a person's life than a good intention or a New Year's resolution. His churches deal with people who are living lives that would be impossible to change unless they genuinely turned themselves over to Jesus Christ.

There are no quick fixes for people like the homeless of New York City. Many of them have lost sight of their own humanity. Their lives are often such a succession of tragic failures and disappointments that they don't even want to risk considering the possibility that things could be different.

So real help for them doesn't come from pretty words. They receive something strong and tangible that they can wrap their arms around and cling to as they fight to regain control of their circumstances. Anything less becomes more quicksand under their feet. Another failed attempt. Another disappointment. Another lie.

The Christians walking around that table full of hungry people every Saturday and talking about Jesus know the reality of the situations they are facing. They know their actions matter as much as their words. And they are willing to be faithful.

This sort of accountability is costly and time-consuming. But when they heard Sam preach that evangelism is a ministry, not a program, these church members believed him enough to make their evangelism a way of life.

"Remember, your hand may be the hand God is looking for to help someone. Your heart may be the heart God wants to love through. Remember, the Messiah has no schedule," they had heard their pastor say many times.

At Wake-Eden another group—comprised mainly of young adults—also took Sam's words to heart. They turn their ministry to people living with a different kind of hopelessness. Every week they leave their safe, comfortable homes for an evening or a day and go into a New York prison to talk about Jesus. Their idea is for young Christians to reach out to young prisoners.

One of the prisons where they go, Riker's Island, houses some of the state's most hardened criminals. The church group passes through several security checks and heavy steel doors before they are allowed to go near the inmates. But once they are inside with the prisoners, they sing, lead a Bible study, pray, and fellowship.

Occasionally Sam accompanies the group to one of their meetings. He never hears the clanging of those heavy doors behind him without thinking about the many kinds of prisons people construct around themselves.

Some of the men he sees sitting inside their locked cells will never leave. They will never hear the prison doors closing behind them. They will never step outside the guarded walls back into society. Physically, they are imprisoned for life.

But a few of them, because of faith in Jesus Christ, have already been freed spiritually. In a very real sense they are much freer than those men who walk the streets of the Bronx every day oblivious to the freedom available through Jesus. That truth is the hope these young people offer those who will never leave the prison, and the rehabilitation for those who will.

Sam is proud of his churches' ministries to the homeless and to the imprisoned. But he is equally happy with the work they do for those whose needs are much more subtle—ordinary, you might even say.

There are many nurses and other health-care workers in his churches, and they have formed a medical fellowship serving both church members and the community. They provide blood pressure screenings, CPR training, health-related seminars, and an annual health fair. Round-the-clock medical attention is also available for those who are very ill.

There is nothing dramatic about this ministry, but it was a significant inroad into the community.

Every Sunday as he preaches Sam sees a reminder of another ministry, as several people quietly slip out of the service. Each week a dedicated few go to five nursing homes and hold worship services for the residents.

Sam has seen many of his members grow as they become involved in these ministries. There was one man who had little confidence in his ability to do anything. He feared standing before a group of people to speak. But Sam saw something in him no one else had seen. He encouraged the man to accompany one of the deacons to the nursing home one Sunday. Then he persuaded him to become the deacon's permanent helper. Every time Sam spoke to the man, he found some small way to build his pride and confidence. When one day on short notice the deacon called to say he could not conduct the nursing home service, Sam managed to talk the helper into doing it. Now he preaches regularly not only at the nursing home, but often in church when Sam is away.

Every year the churches make detailed application to the city for dozens of Youth Corps workers. These young people—black, white, and Hispanic—come to work with day camps and Vacation Bible Schools. They work shoulder to shoulder with the summer missionaries. Sam always reminds the missionaries that these co-workers, as well as the children, are also their missions field.

While the church needs the extra hands, accepting these city youth workers opens the door to many potential problems. More than likely, the majority are not Christians.

Home life for many of them is nonexistent. They often have a mother who doesn't care, and many never see their father. They could be into drugs, gangs, crime, or other trouble. But the church accepts them, happy to provide not only a summer job, but the love of a heavenly Father.

The summer is also a time when both churches and all the missions literally take to the streets to share the gospel. For two months every year, Sunday night services are held outdoors in a nearby parking lot or dead-end street. If people won't come inside to hear about Jesus, the churches will take His story outside. They never change the message, but no method is sacred as they look at a city full of needs.

With such an emphasis on ministry, Bronx Baptist and Wake-Eden found it natural to extend their witness to other parts of the Bronx. They still support a mission in the building on Honeywell Avenue where Bronx Baptist started. They maintain chapels in two other parts of the borough. At different times they have also sponsored prayer groups and Bible studies for targeted groups, such as the Haitians.

In one of their earliest church-planting efforts they helped start a mission in a place called Co-Op City.

Co-Op City is exactly what the name implies—one giant city of apartments. Sam likes to tell visitors to the Bronx that you could be born, live your life, go to two years of junior college and never leave Co-Op City.

It is the most densely populated area in New York City. More than 64,000 families live there. That translates to about 225,000 people. And until Sam helped start a mission there, no evangelical church was located inside that city within a city. Now the church operates completely on its own, with a membership of more than 300 people.

In the process of carrying out other, more routine programs, the churches often uncover individual needs. After weekly cottage prayer meetings, members go into the surrounding neighborhoods for visitation. One night a small group of church members knocked on an apartment door and were greeted by a man who was obviously bothered and distracted. They could see the worry lining his face. He invited them inside, and within moments began spilling out the story of how he had been laid off from his job and wasn't able to find work. He seemed relieved to share with someone, even strangers, his fears about a past due rent bill and no money to buy groceries.

The visitors pooled the money in their pockets and gave him $75. They didn't stop to consider whether the man was preying on their sympathies to get some quick cash. And he could have been. After they left, they went by to tell Sam about the visit. He made a few calls the next day, and through his contacts the man found a job that week.

It wasn't long before he became a Christian and joined the church. He had been a stranger to all of them before that visitation night.

Sometimes the churches minister to people they will never know. This was the case when one of Bronx Baptist's members tearfully shared her fears for a sister with breast cancer. The sick woman did not have insurance and she could not afford a necessary operation. They responded by collecting a love offering.

Several weeks later the church received a thank-you note.

> I cannot say thanks enough to Bronx Baptist Church for its outpouring of Christian love that was so spontaneously displayed during my recent hospitalization. Your more than generous contribution of $3,162 made it possible for me to have a life-saving cancer operation.
>
> Not only do I thank you for your material contri-

bution, but even more so for your prayers which have miraculously brought me through this difficult period. . . .

Lastly, but of primary importance, I must give thanks to God Who in His mercy has touched your hearts of compassion so that you could so lovingly reach out to touch a sister in need.

Sam teaches his churches practicality in their demonstration of Christ's love. If they truly want to minister in a real world, they must be willing to be real people offering a real God. Proclamation alone, he says, will never get the message out.

"Minister as you go," he often tells the churches. He wants them to understand that effective evangelism cannot be programmed. "We must practice it."

He discovered years ago that not everyone would see or agree with his visions for ministry. Sometimes people even offer opposition. Too often a small group of people do the work while the majority sits back.

Sam would acquire federal funds to help pay for the Saturday feeding program, and critics would see the expense of heating and cooling the church that day. A report would be given that 40 had eaten that week and they would say, "What's 40 out of the thousands still out on the streets?" A former convict saved through a prison ministry would speak at the church, and afterwards some would shake their heads at the futility of fighting crime in a city like New York.

Such a lack of vision on the part of fellow Christians is one of the few things that can really make Sam sad. But he is determined that no one will block the outpouring of God's love into the lives of those in need.

"When we think of the mission of the church in the city, immediately we begin to think of lack of personnel, lack of money, lack of facilities, etc. Jesus did not spend His time thinking about the lack of these things; He simply began with the resources at His disposal,'' Sam once wrote.

When faced with those who cannot or will not see the vision, he slowly and quietly looks around and finds other, less obvious, perhaps more passive people to accept the challenge. Over the years he has learned that whenever God gives a vision, He provides the people to help make that vision a reality.

Sam wishes that all his church members, and all Christians, would look to Jesus as their model for ministering in the city.

"He began to preach, to teach, to heal in Galilee, where He was.

"He was knowledgeable of the things He would not do because of the Roman Empire, the things He would not do because of the religious leaders. . . .

"He knew that to preach the good news of the Kingdom in Galilee was not reaching the then known world. To teach a few people on the hillside of Galilee was not reaching all of mankind. To heal the sick and lame was never going to eradicate human diseases. Neither was feeding the 5,000, the 4,000, the removal of world hunger. Jesus, as a member of a minority, an insignificant group of people within a great society, did that which was proper and right to do. He did not wait to do good, for to that end He came to this world,'' Sam said, speaking of the church's mission in the city.

If city Christians really understand their mission, there are some things they have no choice about, Sam believes.

First, they must be obedient in calling people to faith in God through Jesus Christ. That same obedience must continue in meeting spiritual, physical, and mental needs;

and ultimately be a consistent voice calling for righteousness.

Secondly, they must accept the responsibility of speaking out on the issues surrounding them. Abortion, homosexuality, racism, and other such sensitive subjects cannot be taboo for the city Christian. The people who need Jesus Christ the most are themselves the issues.

Finally, Sam believes, the city church must advocate for the poor and speak justice to the rich. Neglecting to deal with such basic moral problems as hunger, poverty, unemployment, housing, and health care is less than honest behavior for the city church. It is shaping Jesus into a narrow human philosophy rather than letting Him loose to touch the hurt of a Christless humanity through His church.

Sometimes, without realizing it, one person will embrace a ministry with such sincerity that they will appear to embody Sam's idea of missions in the city. It is as if the Lord knows when to send those people across Sam's path.

One Thursday night he was chatting with Hyacynthe, a woman who came every week to the midnight prayer meeting. They were talking about the meeting and how it had started.

Back in 1970 Sam was fervently preaching one Sunday morning. Before he knew it, he made the bold proclamation that people needed to go back to all-night prayer meetings.

"You know, sometimes when I preach I get happy," Sam said to Hyacynthe as they laughed about that day. He hadn't planned to call for all-night prayer meetings. He hadn't even thought about it. But he just got carried away, and the idea actually sounded very inspired. Now he wondered sometimes if he had been.

After the service, one of the deacons came to him excited and ready to attend the all-night prayer meetings. When and where would the pastor hold the first one? Sam had indeed started something. But that was all right with him.

The following Thursday night the deacon and several other church members met in the church basement and waited for the pastor to arrive.

He came in a little after eight o'clock, spoke casually to everyone, and sat down. They were all unusually quiet. Small talk quickly died out as Sam took a seat. Everyone instinctively turned and looked at him.

Sam looked back at them.

He was prepared for this face-off. Unspoken expectations hung in the air. He was the pastor. This was a prayer meeting. He should lead.

But he had a different idea. If this prayer group was to have a life of its own, and a purpose of its own, leadership would have to come from those who came to pray. Otherwise, it would just become another meeting and another obligation.

So Sam continued to look back at them just as expectantly as they looked at him. People began to clear their throats and shift in their seats. Finally, one brave soul spoke up and asked, "Should we just start praying now?"

"Brother, I believe that would be an excellent idea," Sam said, and bowed his head.

He and Hyacynthe laughed as they recalled that first meeting. Since that night a core group of 10 to 12 people never miss a Thursday. They decided to meet just until midnight, however, instead of all night.

As Sam and Hyacynthe talked about the meetings, he asked a casual question without even really knowing why.

"Tell me, dear lady, what is it that you pray for every Thursday until midnight?"

"Well, Pastor, I have a tall order for God," she replied.

"Oh, I'm sure you do," Sam said to himself, some of the cynicism of the city creeping into his thinking. How often he heard long lists of personal aches and pains, wants and desires offered up to God—while people all around him were dying in sin.

But Hyacynthe stopped him cold as she finished answering his question.

"I would like Him to fill my heart, so I can be kind to people," she said.

That was it. That was her tall order for God. To fill her heart so she could be kind to people.

Then she began to tell Sam why this request was such a tall order. Her ministry, she had decided, was to the homeless people she passed on the streets. Not the ones who came to the church looking for help, but the ones who didn't even make it that far. She had decided to help the most untouchable people her society had to offer.

"I saw a man sleeping on the subway car, all wrapped up in a dirty blanket. It was dirty as him," she said. The train jerked and wakened him. He opened his eyes and blinked, sitting up and pulling the blanket around his shoulders.

"I kept looking right at him until he finally looked around and his eyes met mine."

That's when she told him to pick himself up and care about himself.

Hyacynthe was certainly no trained psychologist, but she knew he couldn't consider the concept that God loved him if he had never thought about loving himself.

She saw another man living on the street inside a cardboard box. Squatting down so that she could look him in the eye, she asked why he was living that way. He had had an apartment once, he said, but the building burned and he was left with nothing.

Well, now that he was down on the bottom, God would

pick him up, she replied. Then she told him about the Saturday food program.

She was often stern in her approach to the people she met and the stories they told her.

"They could be high or drunk or something. I know they could get mad and hurt me. I do think about that," she said. But she talked to them anyway.

"I just ask the Lord for wisdom and strength."

One day on the subway she saw a woman who looked hungry. So she went up to her and told her about welfare and the Salvation Army.

"I don't want a handout," was the gruff reply.

"Look, I remember the days when I didn't have food on the table. God always provided. I never gave up on myself. You don't give up on yourself," she said as she pressed a $10 bill into the woman's hand.

She was always willing to share, as long as she knew they needed it.

Sam listened to her tell story after story in a quiet, matter-of-fact way.

"Once there was a man on the train, and his nose was running. He was just sitting there, like he didn't even care.

"I looked around and it was like nobody even saw that man. It was like he wasn't even there.

"So I started asking people if they had a napkin. Most of them didn't like it, and just ignored me or gave me a dirty look. Finally someone handed me a crumpled up napkin.

"I just handed it to that man. And you know, he looked at me like I had just handed him a sack of gold.

"God can use anything. And if a napkin's all I've got to give, He'll use it."

Her ministry was to see someone who was invisible to the rest of the world and offer a word of hope. Most of her friends didn't even know she was doing this kind of thing, and if they did, they worried about her safety. But she knew what she was doing, and why, and that was all that really mattered to her.

"I see those people smile, and it makes me feel good," she said.

That was what was in it for her. That was her reward.

She had summed up into one word, Sam realized, all of his sermons and speeches about the mission of the church in the city.

"The mission of the church in the city," he said to himself reverently, "is to care."

Chapter 4

As Sam walked up the steps of the 340 Building he noticed some little girls playing jump rope on the sidewalk.

"Cin-der-ell-a, dressed in yel-low," they chanted, jumping faster and faster to keep up with their song.

Inevitably the chant would soon become too fast, and the girls who were jumping would trip and fall or become tangled in the rope.

That was how life had been in the South Bronx for a long time. The chant of poverty, crime, fire, and flight had grown faster and stronger, faster and stronger until the people caught up in the game of surviving there were certain to eventually stumble. Quitting the game was the only alternative left to far too many of them, Sam decided.

He had seen too many unconcerned landlords abandon buildings with the people still inside, taking no responsibility when water pipes burst and sewage spewed into apartments. Or radiators quit working in the middle of a freezing New York winter. Or swarms of rats came in to further torment frustrated and frightened residents.

He had seen too many mothers huddle with their children on the sidewalk in the middle of the night, crying as they watched their home go up in flames.

He had watched too many poor people lose their dignity

and self-worth because they were denied the basic amenities of human existence.

He had seen too many buildings turn into ugly, vacant shells after the work of an arsonist's torch. Too many streets had become silent graveyards, the skeletons of burned-out buildings left standing to haunt the dying neighborhoods.

He had witnessed too many politicians jump out of a limousine and stand on a street corner surrounded by garbage and rubble—only to make impassioned speeches full of empty promises, and then rush back to their limousines and drive away.

He couldn't stand the thoughts of listening to one more reporter, one more tourist, and especially one more person who lived there, look around and say there was no hope.

Sam has to believe that through His church God can always offer hope, even to a city like New York, in a place called the South Bronx.

No one can point to exactly what happened to bring the South Bronx from being merely a poor neighborhood, as it was in the 1960s, to the devastation of the mid-1970s.

Problems most likely began, Sam believes, when the city failed to respond to a vacuum created by the exodus of middle-class Jews, Irish, and Italians to the suburbs or Co-Op City. Once-thriving apartment buildings began to empty and rents dropped. As the South Bronx quickly changed from middle class to poor, the ethnic mixture became predominately lower-income black and Hispanic. City leaders failed to take adequate action to maintain economic balance in the area.

The rapid deterioration that followed could have been caused by a number of factors. Certainly the loss of nearly one in four manufacturing jobs contributed to the rising level of poverty and the beginning of a South Bronx ghost town. As the jobs began to dwindle, people started to leave. And as people moved out, so did businesses. The downward spiral fed on itself. Between the 1970 and 1980 census, more than 300,000 people fled the South Bronx.

Some people believe some city leaders gave up on the South Bronx community, and actually wanted the area to become a ghost town so they could justify urban renewal. Even the poorest of the poor cannot live with some horrors.

Rent controls made repairs uneconomical for owners, who allowed apartment buildings to undergo gross deterioration. When banks began to redline the area (refuse to grant mortgages), landlords and business owners found it more profitable to torch their buildings and collect the insurance money.

Fear of fire is one of the greatest of many sources of insecurity for poor inner-city residents. The buildings they occupy are often old, poorly constructed, and overcrowded.

Sadly, most of the landlords who burned their buildings did not care about the people trapped inside. Thousands and thousands of fires were deliberately set, in total disregard for the human lives that would certainly be lost.

Social plagues clearly added to the South Bronx debacle. More than 59 percent of the families live on an annual income of less than $10,000. Forty percent of the households depend on welfare payments. Sixty-one percent of the people do not finish high school and one out of four babies is born to a teenaged mother.

In the South Bronx drug dealers sell crack—cocaine—to 12- and 13-year-old children in the hallways of apartment buildings.

People living in these conditions are often overwhelmed by the struggle for their own personal survival and do not care about fighting for the survival of the community.

Sam saw the people trapped inside these issues and knew that they needed a voice, an advocate. City plans, government programs, and political promises had failed them again and again. Even the hope of change brought by the onslaught of national media attention grew sour when the changes didn't come, and a worldwide reputation for death and destruction grew beyond reality.

He could not believe what he was hearing when a friend told him of an article in the *Washington Post* that read:

> An American interviewer defended US democracy to Soviet Foreign Ministry spokesman Gennadi Gerasimov, saying, "We have the American dream. . . . People can be born into poverty. They can escape poverty."
>
> Gerasimov countered, "Suppose you live in the South Bronx? Can you escape poverty in the South Bronx?"

Sam believes you can escape poverty in the South Bronx. But he is a realist. He knows that few can manage such an escape without help. He began to explore every conventional avenue he could think of to provide that help. His churches were open to meeting surrounding needs, but he wanted to go a little deeper. Too often they were just putting bandages on reoccurring problems. Even as he led his churches to help the hungry, the homeless, and the misused, he wanted to do more. Sam wanted to attack the roots of these problems. He wanted to live in a city where there was less hunger, less homelessness, less injustice, and less waste of human life.

He was idealistic enough to believe that there were things he could do to make a difference, even in a city the size of New York. At the same time, he was practical enough to realize that there were many obstacles and limitations. But to Sam each victory is a triumph, large or small. So he worked his way through the channels of government bureaucracy.

His strategy is to first explore all the plans and programs, forms, grants, loans, and licenses offered by the system. There is help available, with certain stipulations, to those who know how to find it. So he spends hour after hour doing paperwork that he hates. Sometimes it pays off. Often it does not. But Sam keeps trying. He might get an extension on someone's electric bill, or free food for Bronx Baptist's Saturday feeding program, or money for one of the preschools.

He has also learned the benefits of becoming a part of the system. If you really want to get some things done, you must make yourself known and available. Often that strategy will place you on controlling boards or agencies.

Many local issues such as housing and sanitation come before the community planning boards. Sam has served on two of them. He has a direct link to local police officers through his membership on the 46th Precinct Council Executive Board.

Issues such as sanitation and police relations are not routine matters for the city poor. Many live in places where there are more rats than people. Dealing with rat-bite fever, illnesses resulting from rabies-infected dog bites, and diseases fostered by unsanitary living conditions are daily occurrences for them.

Also, there are fewer places where police protection is more important than the inner city. Yet this is where there often exists the least understanding and rapport between police and community. The people often view police as unfair and abusive, while the police view the community as hostile and uncooperative.

Not a paid bureaucrat or an elected official, Sam is free to serve on these boards as a real bridge between the people and the system that is supposed to be serving them.

He understands too that knowing somebody never hurts. Wherever he goes and whatever he does, Sam is always making contacts. Sometimes he is late for a meeting with the borough president and doesn't have time to find a parking place on the street. No problem, he knows the attendant at the parking lot marked Full. One extra space can always be found for a friend. Or maybe he wants New York Mayor Ed Koch to write a letter of congratulations for one of his church's anniversary celebration programs. A friend in the mayor's office arranges it.

Through little instances such as these Sam began to realize that more important victories are there to be won.

Big government does not intimidate Sam, nor do the politicians. He knows who he is. And he knows that they, just like he, are human. Some are good, some are bad. Sam learned quickly from living in New York that you can't trust everybody. So he supports and works with the good politicians; many of them are his friends. And while he may want the bad ones out of office, he knows how to deal with them too when necessary.

He understands that clout makes a difference to all politicians. Clout is something he has learned how to use as his leadership in many activities began bringing him a certain amount of influence.

Being president and then chairman of the board of the New York City Council of Churches made him a very prominent voice in the state and at times the nation. And as president of the Baptist Convention of New York, he is an example in the state for the more than 14 million Southern Baptists across the country. Those positions at times give him a strong platform from which to speak.

So through the years Sam has developed the contacts, experience, and political savvy to work effectively within the system. And just as important, he recognizes the times when a problem will not be solved by the system. When that happens, he finds the skills and the courage to step outside the system and create his own solution.

Leaving the system to try a new approach was the path he took when the South Bronx was undergoing the worst of its urban nightmare.

Sam saw thousands of dollars allocated time and time again to urban renewal and model cities, knowing that they would not make a dent in the real needs of the community. He watched that money being wasted, all the while filling out form after form requesting funds.

And perhaps most painful for him to accept was the exclusion of black religious leaders in the search for solutions to the South Bronx's woes. Conferences were held, coalitions were formed—but without the input of area black churches.

Other black ministers experienced the same frustrations. They began to realize that individually their churches were not going to be recognized as viable agents of change for the city.

It became obvious that alone the churches would not get the government money they wanted to help put the community back together. Nor would they have enough influence to make the powers that be listen to their proposals and ideas. This was a disheartening realization for ministers such as Sam. They knew that their churches, perhaps better than anyone, understood the kinds of needs most urgent out in the community.

Somebody, somewhere in this South Bronx cycle of catastrophe had to reinstate trust and integrity. Somehow people needed a decent and safe place to live. If only some of the fear were eliminated, perhaps people could stop running. And when they really could stop running from fire and despair, when they really could stop living in fear and helplessness, then they could turn to their spiritual needs. Sam knew in his heart that these things were true.

Finally, 79 black religious leaders met together to pray, share what they were doing, and talk about what they wanted to do to help the people in the community. Out of this group came the Bronx Shepherds Restoration Corporation. They called themselves Shepherds because they were mostly ministers shepherding (caring for and leading) congregations.

With the help of their churches, they set out as catalysts for change and development throughout the South Bronx. Their commitment was to building a new Bronx where the citizens would have real impact on the future of their community. And after too many years of watching whole groups leave the area en masse, they were committed to maintaining the rich multiracial mix that had long comprised the face of the Bronx.

In a statement of purpose they wrote:

"As destructive as the burning and abandoning of buildings is, the greater devastation is the destruction of human potential and drive for self-realization—the death of the people."

According to Sam, they simply believed that the people of God should become involved wherever people were hurting.

Their highest ambition was to restore life to the Bronx—spiritually and physically. To do this, the Shepherds decided to concentrate on four basic needs—housing, employment, economic development, and evangelism.

The impact of street after street full of buildings crumbling on the outside and gutted on the inside was as demoralizing as anything that had happened to the South Bronx. In all, more than 1,200 buildings had been burned and abandoned.

On some streets the only relief scattered among the ugly

black towers was an occasional vacant lot where a building had been bulldozed. Weeds populated these lots, springing up among pieces of jagged glass and broken bricks.

Charlotte Street, one of the worst burned-out areas, had even been called "a national shame," by President Jimmy Carter in 1977.

The South Bronx looked like the most desolate 18 square miles in America. And, in fact, maybe it was. But Sam insisted to the Shepherds, the city, the state, the federal government, and anybody else who would listen that it was prime real estate.

He quickly pointed out that surrounding those 18 square miles was the rest of the Bronx—the second largest of New York's five boroughs. Approximately 2 million people of all races, nationalities, and cultures live there. Universities, parks, and recreational facilities are plentiful, as are major expressways crisscrossing the borough. Five of them link the Bronx to Manhattan and Long Island.

Sam wanted to see the Shepherds restore that South Bronx real estate. He knew it could be done because he had already been involved in a major building program, before the fires ever began their rampage on the Bronx.

In 1966, just two years after Bronx Baptist Church started, Sam saw the need for housing in the area where the church was located. Before long he led Bronx Baptist to join with some other local churches and a few community organizations in proposing a housing plan to the city planning commission.

The commission accepted the plan and the Twin Parks Housing Association became an official organization. They were to develop new housing and reclaim old buildings in two local park areas. Their major thrust would be to build 3,000 units of new housing including 1,400 low-income units scattered throughout the neighborhood.

They would also make federal, state, and city funds available to private owners who wanted to rehabilitate their buildings.

Few of the association's members had any expertise in what they had set out to do. But they stepped out on faith because, as Sam said, "Not to launch out to meet the desperate housing need around us would be to demonstrate a total lack of concern for human need."

He became treasurer of the association's advisory committee, the liaison between the community and various funding agencies. City, state, federal, and private agencies provided funds. The New York State Urban Development Corporation became the developers.

The main responsibility of the advisory committee was to put together a package of community needs—housing, schools, recreational facilities, day-care centers.

Hour after hour was spent in meetings with lawyers, builders, draftsmen, agency representatives, and other specialists. There were community meetings, private hearings, public hearings, and always information to be gathered and presentations to be prepared.

"The road up the mountain is sometimes winding but when the top is reached and the mission is accomplished, the view is beautiful," Sam wrote of the experience.

His knowledge of working the system was infinitely multiplied through this process. He later found his work on this committee invaluable as he led in organizing the Shepherds.

When construction of the new buildings actually began in 1970, Sam could hardly stay away from the sites.

"When one could watch these skyscrapers decorating the communities, they seemed to say to each one of us, 'New hope, new life, new housing for many, and for many others better housing,' " he told one group.

But there was little time to take in the miracle he saw

being built before his eyes. A tenant selection committee came up with guidelines and standards that would be used to screen tenant applications. Sam was chairman of that committee. They were soon swamped with more than 14,000 applications for 3,000 apartments.

The selection of tenants was dictated in part by law and in part by the association's plan to renew hope among the people in the community. First priority was given to the people who had been moved out to make way for the new buildings. Twin Parks did not intend to be an urban renewal project that further displaced the people it was supposed to be helping. The next priority group, according to law, included Vietnam veterans, people from within the postal area, and people from within the borough. The last group was anyone who could afford the rent.

Sam met with new tenants of the buildings, witnessed to them, and offered himself as their pastor. Each family received a Bible bearing the message:

> Welcome to your new community. We trust that under God we can build a strong and godly community. If ever the church can be of help to you, do not hesitate to call the church at 933-4095.
> Your pastor, Sam Simpson

The church couldn't handle the telephone calls that followed.

Bronx Baptist began to see the ministry opportunities unfolding, especially in the buildings nearest the church. Some members who needed apartments moved into the new buildings. They began organizing prayer meetings with other new tenants. Other church members began showing Saturday morning movies for children in one building's recreation room. A youth group organized in another building. Door-to-door witnessing and visitation among the tenants became an organized church effort. They also opened the church building for all kinds of community meetings.

The association had come full circle. People found homes, and in the process the church became an important part of many lives. At least in the new and refurbished buildings provided by Twin Parks, hope had been introduced on a physical and spiritual level.

By the time the Shepherds organized in 1978, Sam knew exactly what he wanted to see accomplished in the ongoing struggle to save the South Bronx. As the Shepherds considered where to begin their housing program, he knew that the strongest areas left were the ones right around their churches. Because the churches stayed even when banks and businesses closed their doors, they had become the remaining symbol of normal community. So the Shepherds looked close to home when they began seeking out nearby buildings for renovation.

They knew too well that for all their plans, without money they couldn't do a thing. Even with funds from the state of New York, New York City, and various individuals, they faced staggering housing rehabilitation costs.

City planners and housing specialists who met with them were quick to point out that at approximately $50,000 per unit, they wouldn't be able to do much renovation. But the Shepherds had a plan that they hoped would take care of that problem. They called it sweat evangelism.

They decided to ask church members to tithe five days of their time per year to work on the housing rehab projects. Sam provided access to a giant labor force by enlisting teams of Southern Baptist volunteers to participate in the sweat evangelism plan.

The bottom line was that the tithed labor would bring that $50,000 refurbishing cost down to about $10,000. Those figures alone made their neighborhood revitalization program more attractive to potential investors and developers. And on a larger scale, when a 20-unit building was rehabilitated for $200,000 instead of $1,000,000 through tithed labor, the Shepherds still retained a "sweat equity" investment of $800,000. That investment would be there later when they were in a position to use it.

As the Shepherds began to define their identity, Sam talked with his contacts at the Home Mission Board to explore the possibility of tying into Southern Baptist urban evangelism plans.

Key home mission strategists came to New York to meet with the Shepherds. They spent more than 12 hours talking about the plight of the Bronx, and how the Shepherds planned to help. They walked around neighborhoods and saw for themselves the devastating need.

They listened to Sam's argument that you cannot evangelize a man's soul and leave out his body.

After the meeting they agreed to give Southern Baptist support to the Shepherds. In a follow-up report they wrote:

> We believe that Bold Mission Thrust demands our openness to new relationships, new avenues of wisdom, and new opportunities of mobilizing the laity in mission. This opportunity of relationship with a large indigenous group in the nation's largest city must be evaluated in the light of God's providential moving in our denomination. We feel that God is in this and that He expects us to respond faithfully to this opportunity.

Soon two Southern Baptist laymen, a retired lawyer and a land developer, were recruited to serve as consultants for the group. Some Southern Baptist churches and laypersons pledged funds.

Sam found this response from his denomination affirming on two very personal levels.

First, it showed him a growing awareness in an area he had long found weak among Southern Baptists. He could not distinguish between evangelism and social involvement, but that was often what he saw happening in his denomination. Experience had proven that on his missions field it was impossible to evangelize without ministering. As a home missionary, it felt good to know that the people supporting him could understand the realities of an effective city ministry.

And then something about seeing white Southern Baptist leaders come to his territory to meet with black religious leaders made a statement to Sam about changing racial attitudes. Too many times he had seen blacks and other ethnic groups excluded from the heart of denominational decision making.

"Although we sing together 'We are one in the bond of love,' we practice we are two in the bond of service," Sam had once told participants of an evangelism conference.

"We talk about evangelizing metropolitan areas, yet we treat the residents we want to minister to as children. We make the decisions for them. We print and take the program to them. It won't work if evangelism is to be effective. Include them in your planning and take their suggestions and use some."

Sam has seen many attitudes grow and change over the years, as more and more Southern Baptists came to the Bronx to participate in the Shepherd's sweat evangelism.

The Shepherds took all the help they could get; and year by year refurbished not only apartment buildings, but schools, churches, and businesses. Each person who took residence in one of their new buildings was witnessed and ministered to consistently. They expanded their community development beyond housing.

With a grant from the borough president they began a youth development program that trained high school dropouts in building maintenance and repair. Besides giving them a marketable skill, the program taught discipline and motivation. They were also given remedial lessons in reading, math, science, and social studies. These classes provided the preparation they needed for the GED (general equivalency diploma) exam. When the participants were ready to leave the program they received help with interview techniques, filling out job applications, writing a resumé, and exhibiting proper work habits.

In the summer the Shepherds gave at least ten youth workers eight weeks of employment. Again, many of these kids had not been exposed to the world of work and learned some basic, practical skills.

Some of these youth worked on a state-funded Shepherd's program to weatherize apartments occupied by elderly or handicapped tenants. By replacing doors, windows, ceilings, flooring, and various types of building insulation, they made winters a little more bearable for people who couldn't afford to move to a better apartment.

Shepherds work that could not be done by volunteers was given to local contractors whenever possible. They knew exactly where all their money was going, and funneled as much of it as possible back into the community.

Now Sam could drive through the South Bronx and see physical signs of hope scattered among the burned-out buildings that for so long dominated an urban wasteland. New laws delaying insurance payments for suspicious blazes had, for the most part, stopped the fires. New and refurbished buildings began to elbow their way onto streets long dominated by emptiness and abandonment.

Slowly, the burned-out Bronx building was becoming a reminder of a sickening past, not a signpost of an empty future.

At least six of those new-faced buildings were there because the Shepherds Restoration Corporation had come into being. They manage those six buildings and own another one.

The purchase of their own property, which they proudly call the 340 Building because of the address, is the greatest milestone the group has achieved. Their ultimate goal is to become totally independent of government funds. The equity potential offered in this 66-unit building is a giant step in that direction.

But whether they own or manage the buildings, Sam knows that inside something is different from any other apartment building in New York City.

Inside the Shepherds buildings every single person has heard a word about Jesus. Every person has seen His love demonstrated every day through the ministry of some church member. And most markedly personal, every man, woman, and child living in one of those buildings has already experienced His power to change physical lives. They have a home because Jesus made it happen.

Sam knows that each piece of sheetrock hung, each drop of paint used, each nail hammered, each brick replaced represents a prayer that those people would give Jesus the power to change their hearts as He is changing the Bronx.

Chapter 5

"Hey, take a picture of that graffiti over there. I can't believe I don't have my camera!"

"I want to get one of the wash hanging out the windows."

"What are all those burned-up cars doing sitting on the sidewalks? I mean, do people just leave them there?"

"Oh, gross! Look at that man digging through the garbage can. What's he doing?"

Sam was taking four of the summer missionaries to Bronx Baptist in the church van, and had stopped by the 340 Building on the way. After almost two weeks in the Bronx, this was their first trip, other than by subway, out of the comfortable neighborhoods surrounding Wake-Eden. At last they were seeing a side of the city that they had expected.

Hearing their comments, Sam decided they should take a little tour of the South Bronx.

"So what do you think of our fair city, eh?" Sam asked over his shoulder.

"Look! There's another guy washing his car in the street. I mean, let's just get out a box of laundry detergent and pretend we're at the carwash. How come everybody washes their cars right in the middle of the street?" one of them asked.

"Well, that's the only place they have to do it. There aren't any yards or driveways in this neighborhood."

"We're going to die!" one of the girls shrieked in mock terror, grabbing the girl beside her, as Sam braked suddenly. They were behind a car that stopped to let a passenger out on the sidewalk.

"Why do all New Yorkers just stop in the middle of the street? I mean, let's just park right here. Forget 65 lanes of traffic flying up behind us," the same girl said. They all laughed at what had apparently already become a group joke—"those crazy New York drivers."

Sam just looked in the rearview mirror and smiled.

"Would you like to see a little of the South Bronx?" he asked, making a left turn that would take them toward Charlotte Street.

"Sure," they all said, not really aware of the significance of what they would be seeing. Right now they were sorry that only one of them had brought along a camera this morning.

"Look over here, quick! There's some great graffiti on that wall. Hurry, get your camera out," one of the girls said.

As she looked up past the graffiti to the gaping windows and charred interior she asked, "Pastor, how come all these buildings look like they've been burned inside? They're so ugly, I mean, why doesn't the city just tear them down?"

"Well, because they're perfectly good buildings. They just need to be gut-rehabed."

"Gut what?" one of the boys asked as he looked for the automatic rewind button on his new camera.

"Gut-rehab. The buildings have been gutted by fire on the inside, but the outside structure is still sound. When you go in and rehabilitate one of these buildings, it's called a gut-rehab building."

"Wouldn't it be easier to just start over from scratch?" someone asked. "I mean, look at that one. It looks like it's been bombed."

"Well, look right next-door. See that nice new looking building? It's a gut-rehab job. The cost would have been much much greater to, as you say, 'start from scratch,' " Sam replied.

"And with all the buildings that have burned in the Bronx during the past 20 years, well, you just have to do what you can," he added.

He drove slower so they could better see the buildings as he pointed to them.

"This South Bronx is a much different one than you would have found just a few years ago," Sam said.

"What do you mean?"

"Well, the main thing is that the fires have stopped."

"Fires?"

"Yes, the South Bronx was brought to its knees by a long series of terrible fires," Sam said, and proceeded to give them a condensed but powerful history lesson on the area.

By the time he stopped the van at Charlotte Street, they could almost see the flames and smell the smoke that for so many years engulfed the South Bronx.

"And many people died in those terrible fires," Sam finished, turning around to find them all leaning forward to hear his words.

"This is Charlotte Street. Have any of you ever heard of it?" he asked, helping the girls step out onto the sidewalk. None of them had.

"Well, you need to take a picture of this street," he said to the boy with the camera. "Some people you might consider pretty important have been here."

He told them about the day President Jimmy Carter surprised the South Bronx by coming to stand on Charlotte

Street and promise his help. Sam told about help that filtered down out of that visit, and also the help that never came. They were impressed to hear that they might be standing where Edward Kennedy, Ronald Reagan, Mother Teresa, or Pope John Paul II had once stood.

Sam told them one newspaper had even said a trip to the South Bronx was "as crucial to the understanding of American urban life as a visit to Auschwitz is to understanding Nazism."

As they stood under a sign that read Charlotte Street and had their picture made, they looked around and saw things through slightly different eyes. Insights were deeper, and some of the questions more thoughtful. They didn't realize it, but those four young people were a little more mature in their thinking and outlook after just a brief tour of the South Bronx.

Things were more subdued in the van as they made their way on to Bronx Baptist. The missionaries seemed to be looking past the buildings to the people inside.

"Can you believe that? Look at that woman over there, leaning out her window. The whole bottom floor of her building is burned out. See the boards on the windows?"

"How can she live in a place like that, Pastor?"

"Well, she probably can't afford to move. But from the looks of that building, unless someone comes in and does some rehab work she'll be out before long, one way or another," he said.

Who was doing something, they wanted to know, if the city, the state, and the federal government weren't doing enough? Who else did these people have to turn to?

Sam told them there were many groups and coalitions who had worked for a long time to help where government left gaps. He told them about the Shepherds and what they were doing. And he told them about a rich Southern Baptist legacy born in the South Bronx.

"You're from a long line of sweat evangelists, you know," he said, grinning, waiting for the anticipated jokes from the young missionaries. After they made their attempts to define his term, Sam began to explain how Southern Baptist sweat evangelism had been instrumental in the Shepherds' work. Fascinated, they listened as he told story after story about the people who came to the Bronx before them. Most of the people he talked about came strictly to rebuild buildings. Some, like them, came as missionaries, others as part of youth groups or choir tours. But all of them found a place of unique ministry in the South Bronx setting.

Sweat evangelism is one of the most successful projects Sam has ever seen put into practice. Through the years, thousands of volunteers from every state in the Union have come to the Bronx. At least 1,000 had been involved in the Shepherds' building projects. Working with these groups has been a sweet experience for Sam. He has seen them greatly used by God, and seen God move among them.

The very first sweat evangelists to come were from Virginia. Part of an associational Brotherhood group, they were typical, ordinary Southern Baptist men. Doing missions work in a New York City slum was like going to a foreign country for them. The area's reputation for poverty and crime made them a little apprehensive. But they were committed to sharing what skills they had with a group called the Bronx Shepherds Restoration Corporation.

They read newspaper and magazine articles about the South Bronx, and watched graphic television reports that left little to the imagination. While they nervously joked about what they might find when they got there, they believed they had prepared. They were ready, they thought, to see for themselves what the South Bronx really had to offer.

And they were stunned.

"We saw a greater need than we had imagined and conditions were worse than we had imagined. As the men saw the run-down buildings they really didn't know what to say. They were speechless," the group's leader said later.

But as they began to work, the men slowly lost the feeling of being overwhelmed. They saw that what they were doing really would make a difference.

They too began to look past the buildings to the people. Every day for a week they did the dirty work of repairing deteriorated Bronx housing. As they worked, people became curious about what they were doing. A group of white, southern men singing about Jesus as they rebuilt apartments in a predominantly black and Hispanic neighborhood was, to say the least, quite an unusual sight.

After all they had heard and seen about the South Bronx, the men expected the people to be suspicious or defensive, even hostile. A few of those perceptions began to change as they discovered people who didn't fit the molds. Some passersby would even stop the men on the street to ask what was going on.

And when someone asked, the men were happy to tell. They put down their hammers and paint brushes more than once to explain that they were there because Jesus loved people in the South Bronx just like He loved people in Virginia.

"The people there couldn't believe we were volunteering. They could not believe we would come and work without pay. This really impressed them," the leader said.

The group also impressed city officials at a special breakfast meeting. Three officials who were not Christians were amazed at the concept of why the group was there. They listened intently as each group member shared his testimony and a little about himself.

They went back to Virginia after a week, but left New York as changed men. Never again would they see New York City as an impenetrable fortress of sin and hopelessness. They knew from experience the difference individual Christians could make. They found a foothold, and prepared the way for others to do the same.

Later groups echoed the feelings of those first few men. They would come to the Bronx a little afraid, and register shock at the devastated conditions, especially the buildings where they would be working. But they would lose their fear as they became involved in the projects.

They found that all they really needed was a heart to help people. Even skill in construction work wasn't a must, as one certified public accountant from Tennessee discovered. He felt a lot better about his unfamiliar role as carpenter when he saw the building where his group would be working.

"Surely," he thought, "there's nothing even I can do to hurt that building."

Time after time the volunteers voiced a desire to reclaim lives as they reclaimed buildings.

That same inexperienced CPA from Tennessee witnessed to six different people during his visit. One black man named Jose told him that he had "never heard anyone talk about God like him."

What those men actually did, according to Sam, was come to the Bronx, touch people, and say "I love you." For some volunteers, reaching far enough to touch the people of the Bronx was a longer stretch than they ever imagined.

One white Southern Baptist businessman was asked by people at home why he would want to go all the way to New York, when there were poor blacks "on the other side of the tracks'' in his own hometown. While he did not agree with this mentality, he had in his own mind limited how God could use him. His background and up-bringing, he thought, would make such a ministry to blacks impossible where he lived. He could, however, accept going to the Bronx to share Christ's love.

But when he got there, he began to realize that, for all their racial and cultural differences, the blacks in New York's Bronx weren't that different from him. Not really. Not when it came to what was important. And that had to mean that neither were the blacks in his hometown.

Sam summed up some newfound feelings for that businessman as he spoke to the group just before they left for home.

''If we have achieved nothing more from this visit, we have made some white people come to terms with the fact that blacks are real people capable of responding to love and reciprocating love,'' he said.

The man thought about these words. That week he had been able to look out into a sea of black faces and say ''I love you'' and mean it. He had seen the people behind those faces. In this setting, the color of someone's skin truly did not matter.

But he was going home. There wouldn't be anything exotic or unusual about the poor people where he lived—black or white. Ministering to them would still hold the same problems, pitfalls, and possibly backlash. But he took home a new kind of respect for those people, and a new desire to help.

As whites found their attitudes changing toward blacks, so were black attitudes changing toward whites. The testimony of white Southern Baptists coming out of their element to work just for the love of Jesus proved powerful.

When a Bronx city councilman met with one group, he told them, ''You people coming in to a black community and working with us, coming right here and living among the neighborhood people is another way of saying people are the same whether they are black, white, or Hispanic. The quicker we understand that, the quicker we are going to solve race problems.''

So in the Bronx and in the lives of the volunteers, God used sweat evangelism for much more than its original purpose. One minister of music from North Carolina wrote to Sam after he got home.

''We have all unpacked our clothes, told and retold our stories about our week in the Bronx, picked up our developed films, and now we have had time for reflection on what was accomplished and how our lives have been altered by seeing firsthand the missions work in the Bronx. Like most things of true value, our week in New York increases in value to us as time passes.''

Sam never knows what might spark someone's interest in working in the Bronx. One day he got a call from a Southern Baptist layman in New York City on business. He had heard of Sam Simpson and his work in the Bronx, and wanted to see for himself. He met with Sam, saw what his work was all about, and then met with the Shepherds' Executive Committee. He offered some of his advice and business guidance, and then went home to share with his church what he had learned.

Once a group of college students was motivated to work in the Bronx because of a speech Sam gave at a Southern Baptist Theological Seminary conference. As he looked into 700 young faces and talked about the economic and spiritual necessity for missions work in the Bronx, he didn't know that 26 students from Kentucky would respond. But they did.

Eventually they traveled 18 hours on a bus, arrived in the Bronx on New Year's Eve, and spent the following week experiencing the sweat evangelism they had heard about. They worked on painting and reconstruction for the Shepherds, helped with the day schools at Sam's churches, visited in nursing homes, and distributed Bibles in the neighborhood.

Sam loves to talk about the people who come to help in the Bronx. He has seen so much happen. It is as if each person in each group is an individual blessing that just keeps on multiplying. Over and over God has proven that He will be faithful in providing the people to help carry out His ministries.

And sometimes, He might just send somebody that will fill more than a gap in the ministry. Sometimes He will send a volunteer or two that will fill a space in the heart.

That was how Sam felt about Ray and Frances Boggs. Surely his relationship with them exemplified the amazing ability God could give His workers to transcend earthly differences. Without the love of Jesus Christ, this black Jamaican city pastor would surely have had little in common with a retired white man from Okeechobee, Florida, who was a recovered alcoholic. But God brought the two of them together, and they loved each other like brothers.

When the Boggses first began to consider going to the Bronx as Mission Service Corps workers, they heard all kinds of objections to their plans. Friends and relatives reminded them in graphic detail about the violence, racial tension, muggings, rape, and other dangers waiting for them in New York City. Some even said they were crazy for wanting to go there.

But Ray and Frances Boggs held a vision of what God wanted them to do in the Bronx. They felt that the ministries they saw there were of Him, and they wanted to be a part of that work. So they prayed, asking for God's direction. He answered by giving both of them a feeling of complete peace. From that moment on, there was never another question about fear for either one of them. They knew God had a place for them in the Bronx.

Their only problem was actually being present to do the work. Because of administration duties at a drug and alcohol rehabilitation center there in Florida, staying in New York full time was out of the question. So every month for almost a year they drove 1,274 miles one-way to the Bronx. It was not an easy trip, but every time they returned they were reaffirmed in their commitment to the work there. It was just like going home.

While Frances was busy falling in love with the children of Wake-Eden Christian Academy, Ray would put on his overalls and comfortable shoes, and go to whichever Shepherds building was currently under renovation. He shared a lifetime of contracting experience with the Shepherds. Whatever job needed to be done, they could count on him to show them how.

One day he would be a carpenter, the next a roofer. One day he would repair windows and doors, the next he would install insulation, weatherstripping, plumbing. When there were city codes and requirements to be considered, the Shepherds began looking to Ray Boggs for guidance; he always seemed to know what to do.

He proved especially helpful when other Southern Baptists came to work on one of the buildings. Ray was always right in the middle of the project with them, offering support, helping them work, and sharing his perspective of the people in the Bronx.

For all his help with the actual construction work, Ray's greatest impact was in just being a Christian. His best gift seemed to be seeing past skin color into hearts.

"Many people are really seeking and wanting to change, but they've got no hope," he would say as he perched on a ladder painting a ceiling. Sometimes the men stopped what they were doing just to listen to him.

"They've been oppressed and put down all their lives,

not only by alcohol and drugs, but also by social and physical problems," he would continue.

They would talk about the lost people who might occupy the apartment they were repairing, or the children that might come to the church they were working on. Ray didn't see anything complicated about the Christian's duty when it came to these people.

"It's our responsibility to encourage and train them. If we do this, they'll become Christians."

If sweat evangelism could have been invented for just one person, it surely would have been Ray Boggs, Sam thought. Nothing seemed more natural to Ray than pushing a paintbrush and talking about Jesus.

One day while he was helping with some renovation at a local Baptist church, he noticed a young woman standing nearby watching. He kept working for a few minutes, but began to get the feeling she was there for a reason. She looked like she might need to talk to someone.

Climbing down off the ladder, he pulled a rag out from his pocket and wiped his hands before walking up to the woman and introducing himself. His southern drawl was always an asset when it came to breaking the ice with some stranger in New York.

They began to talk, and before long the woman began crying. Nothing about life was good as far as she was concerned. She had been an alcoholic since she was nine years old. Nobody cared, there was nobody to help. All she knew was pain and disappointment. After years of struggling to survive, there didn't seem to be much point anymore. Her own hopelessness overwhelmed her.

The woman went on and on, pouring her heart out. And Ray Boggs did something no one else had ever really done for that woman in her whole miserable life. He listened to her. He stopped what he was doing, cleared off a place among the paint cans and dropcloths, and sat down and listened to all her problems.

Then he told her that everyone had hope. He told her about his 15 years as an alcoholic. He told her how Jesus saved him.

For nearly two hours they sat there in the middle of the paint and equipment, reading the Scriptures and praying. It was there that he led her to know Christ.

The van had been parked in front of Bronx Baptist Church ever since Sam began talking about Ray Boggs, but none of the missionaries even noticed that they had stopped. Sam captivated them with his stories. One of the girls reached into her purse for a tissue.

"Where are the Boggses now, Pastor? They're not still driving up here every month, are they?" one of the boys asked.

"No. Unfortunately for the Bronx, God called them to help their son staff a home for handicapped and retarded men in Montana. They did that as long as they were needed, and now they live in Colorado," Sam said.

They all said they wished the Boggses were still in the Bronx.

"You know, your being here is an answer to Ray Boggs's prayers," Sam said.

They wanted to know how, in what way.

"Because Ray prayed that people would continue to build bridges and establish relationships that would help people see that there are Christians who love and care for the Bronx. This summer, you will be doing just that."

The missionaries sat there looking at Sam for a few minutes. They all felt a strange kind of closeness.

"You know, my friends," Sam said, "if I have to think of a hero, other than Jesus Christ, it has to be someone like Ray Boggs, or Frances. They are just ordinary people, but look at the extraordinary things they are allowing God to do with them."

Sam surprised himself by making such a revealing statement to this group of young people. So he did what he always does when things get a little too personal. He made a joke.

"Well, because of me you are all late. Shall I write you a hall pass?" he said, moving to open the door.

The spell was broken. The missionaries gathered up their things and stretched as they started to get up. Suddenly one of them remembered that she had been voted spokesperson for the group in a miniconference they held while waiting for Sam outside the 340 Building.

Sam had promised a meeting with them over a week ago. They still didn't know exactly where they were supposed to get the money for groceries, and that was fast becoming a major concern. The only food left in the Wake-Eden house where they were staying was tuna fish and crackers. One sacrifice they had not planned on making this summer was starving.

"Pastor," she said, catching Sam's shirt sleeve as he was about to escape into the church. "When are we going to have our orientation meeting? You promised last week."

"Oh, yes, you're right, I did. We were going to meet that night, what was it, Tuesday? That was the night I had an unexpected meeting. I'm sorry," he said, looking from face to face as the missionaries gathered around him.

"I tell you what. Tonight. We'll do it tonight. No, I can't. I already have another meeting."

Sam looked at the silent faces.

"Well, we'll just do it after my meeting. That's a good idea. After my meeting, say, around 8:30 or 9:00 tonight, you all come to my house. You remember where my house is?" he asked, looking at one of the boys who had been by there one day with him.

"Yes."

"Good, good. Then you tell the others, and I'll see you

all tonight. We'll have a great time, OK? See you tonight then," he said, running down the steps to the basement of the church.

"Yea, Amy!" they all cheered, as soon as the door closed behind him. They were happy that at last one of them had had the nerve to get the pastor to set a specific time.

"Come on, we'd better get going. We're late enough as it is," one of the girls said, opening the door to the church basement.

Everyone ran inside except Amy, who stood on the sidewalk beside the church, just looking around. This was her first day to work at Bronx Baptist. She had been working at Wake-Eden, but today one of the teachers was sick here, so she came to fill in. She had only been here once before—on Sunday, for church. That day, she had been so new and so nervous she didn't really notice the neighborhood.

Bronx Baptist was definitely in a much poorer area than Wake-Eden. It looked like inner city here. High-rise apartment buildings surrounded the church. Everything looked older and dirtier. Even the people seemed different.

As she looked around, Amy thought about all the things Sam had told them. She looked up at the apartment windows, and wondered about the people behind them. She was still standing there staring up at those windows, her eyes shaded against the sun, when one of the boys came outside to get her. "Amy, come on. They're getting ready to divide the classes," he said. "What are you doing?"

"Oh, just looking around," she said.

"Well, come on. They're waiting on us."

She didn't make a move to go with him, turning instead to look in the other direction.

"Have you noticed that there's a burned-out building

across the street from the church? No, look. There are three that have burned,'' she said.

He walked up the steps and stood beside her. How strange, he thought, that he had come here every day last week and not noticed something as obvious as that.

They both stood there thinking the same thoughts for a few seconds.

''I wonder what happened to those people,'' Amy said as they turned to go down the steps to the church.

Chapter 6

Sam started taking off his tie before he came in the
door. It had been a long, long day, and all he wanted to
do was change clothes, eat dinner, and then sit down to
read the newspaper. He knew Lola must be home; he
could smell something cooking. It was after eight o'clock.

"Lols, you are an excellent wife! How did you know
I'd come home tired and without having had any dinner
at this late hour?" he asked, catching her around the waist
and giving her a kiss on the cheek.

"I just had a feeling, Sam," she said, bending over to
clear some books off the dining room table. "How was
your day?"

"Great. It was a great day," he said absently, thumbing
through a large stack of mail and telephone messages.

A tiny little chihuahua begging for attention barked and
jumped up and down around Sam's feet.

"Hello, B.J.," he said, picking up the dog and patting
him on the head.

Just then he turned around and noticed Kim and her
boyfriend sitting on the couch, eating ice cream and gig-
gling at some private joke. He spoke to them.

As the boy stood up to shake hands, Sam thought of
his conversation with Kim just last week.

He had told her she wasn't ready to be so serious with one boy. Sam didn't have anything against her boyfriend. He just hated to see her get too focused on any one person. Still, having one boyfriend had its advantages, as did having several. He really wasn't sure what was best.

Dealing with his children, especially as teenagers, was one of the few areas of uncertainty in Sam's life. Sometimes he just didn't know the right thing to say or do. It was never that they weren't important to him. But with so much to be done and so many needs to be met, matters that demanded immediate attention were always taking him away from their more routine, daily problems.

For years he and Lola had assumed that if parents gave their children the basics—food to eat, clothes to wear, a roof over their heads—in the atmosphere of a good Christian home, a good relationship would naturally develop. But as all three of their children grew, they learned that even for good Christian families with good Christian children, even for families of missionaries and preachers, those relationships are the hardest to build, and often take the most work.

But he was trying. When the children were small he often took them with him to meetings, conferences, or wherever they might just enjoy being along. All three of them had loved these special times alone with their father. They adored him, and their relationships with him were loving and fun. It had been easier for him to fit them into his schedule when they were children than it was for him to fit into theirs when they became teens.

Now he would make dates with them for dinner or lunch, offer to drive them to meet an appointment, or just try to find a time to sit down and talk.

"I still owe Kimmy a dinner," he was thinking when the doorbell rang.

"Can you get that, Sam? I think it's your brother," Lola said from the kitchen.

Ted Jefferson stood at the door. He needed Sam's signature on a legal document for the Shepherds.

"Ted! I thought you were on your way home when I left you at five o'clock."

"So did my wife. But it's been one thing after another, and, well, you know how it is."

"Yes I do."

"Hello, Ted," Lola said, moving some more books to put another place mat and plate on the table. "Sit down and have a bite to eat with us."

"Well, I probably ought to be going home," he said, following her into the kitchen as the doorbell rang again. "What smells so good?"

Sam went to the door again to greet his brother, his wife, and their two children. B.J. ran barking through the house with the squealing children chasing him.

Sam introduced his brother to Ted, and the three of them began to talk. The women were in the kitchen discussing whether Lola's roast was ready, while the children ran back and forth in between the two groups, chasing the dog and asking for a peanut butter and jelly sandwich.

As he sat at the table nibbling on some lettuce, Sam kicked his shoes off and leaned back in his chair. He loved times like this when his house was filled with people. Everyone was laughing and happy, and the smells of a spicy roast filled the air. This was how he remembered his childhood home in rural Jamaica—a blur of activity, with people always coming and going and sharing meals with his family.

His brother had come by to talk about their mother's upcoming visit to New York. Sam had made all the arrangements. She would be arriving in a couple of weeks. Their conversation was interrupted by the ringing of the telephone. It was a long-distance call for Sam.

As he put one hand over his ear to hear, Lola began setting the food on the table. Ted decided to stay, but Sam's brother and his wife said they had to go and get their children ready for bed. Sam continued to talk, and waved as they went to the door.

B.J. started whining and dancing around the table on his hind legs as soon as Lola took the roast out of the oven.

When Sam hung up the phone, they finally said a blessing and began to eat. As they talked about his mother's visit, Ted asked how long it had been since they visited Jamaica. One topic led to another, and soon they were telling Ted, a native New Yorker, about their homeland. The more they talked, the more they reminisced about old times.

"So how did you two meet? Was it in Jamaica or here in the States?" Ted asked.

"How did we meet? Let me tell you what happened. It was in Jamaica," Sam said.

"I saw this good looking lady running around town, and I said to myself, 'She's going to be my woman.' "

"Ooh!" Lola laughed and groaned at the same time. She knew Sam was really getting ready to tell Ted a story.

"Love at first sight?" Ted asked, laughing.

"Um hmm. And I kept on watching her."

"Patience," Ted said, giving Lola a knowing look.

"Patience," she answered. Sam was famous for his endless, sometimes maddening, patience.

He ignored them.

"So I'd watch her walk up and down King Street, up and down with her friends. She'd go in a restaurant and sit down, I'd go in. Finally, I realized I knew her cousin, so I decided to make friends with him." he said.

"Sam, you must have been a born networker," Ted said.

They were laughing when Kim came up to the table.

"Mommy."

"Kim, please pour Mr. Jefferson some more tea. Your daddy is telling us quite an interesting story."

"Mommy, I wanted to know if we could go to the movies, please," Kim said as she filled the empty glasses with tea.

"What movie? You've already missed the starting time," Lola said.

"No, we wanted to go to the 9:00," Kim answered.

"No. It's too late. You wouldn't be home until after 11:00."

"But Mommy."

"Kim, no. You should have gone earlier if you wanted to see a movie. You were out late last night."

Kim and her mother looked at each other for just a moment before Kim turned around and sat down on the couch.

"Kim," Lola said, but there was no reply, and they both just let it drop. In a few minutes her boyfriend said a quick good-bye to the adults and left. She went into her room and closed the door.

Just as they had resumed their conversation, the doorbell rang again.

"Who is that?" Lola asked.

Looking at his watch, Sam suddenly remembered. It was 9:10.

"I forgot. The summer missionaries are coming tonight for an orientation meeting. It must be them," he said, as he went to the door.

"Hello, young people! Welcome!" Sam boomed as he ushered the eight college students in and introduced them to Ted. They knew Lola from church.

"We're just finishing a late dinner. Sit down and make yourselves at home. I'll be with you in a few minutes," he said, ushering them into the living room.

They quickly took over the room as only a group of college students can, lying on both couches and sitting crossed-legged in the floor. This group looked as if they would be at home wherever they went. There was a lot of laughing and whispering at first. But in just a few minutes they took out their Bibles to have their devotion time while they waited on Sam.

He went back to the table and sat down.

"What were we talking about?" he asked.

"Many things, Sam, many things," Lola said.

Picking up his fork he said quietly, "I don't feel like having an orientation meeting tonight. I'm too tired."

He usually liked to take the new group of summer missionaries out to dinner for this type of meeting, along with some of the church leaders. But that just hadn't worked out this year, and they really did need to be oriented. He could hear them in the background, earnestly discussing the meaning of a particular Scripture passage. No, he couldn't get out of this meeting tonight. He'd just have to go through with it, tired or not.

They finished dinner about the same time the missionaries ended their Bible study. Ted said good-bye, and Sam pulled his chair into the living room.

"Well, now, how are you all tonight? How are you enjoying life in the Bronx?" he asked.

They had lots of impressions to share with him. Everyone began to talk at once, becoming more animated and comical as they added to each other's stories. He couldn't decide if they were more amazed by the two women they saw fighting at the grocery store or a rat that had supposedly run through an attic bedroom at the Wake-Eden house. The girls were particularly carried away with the story about the rat.

Sam sat back and listened, amused at their youthful observations about his city.

"I just want to see a street gang. That would be so cool," one of the girls said. She had been saying this for a week, and it had become a sort of joke among the group.

"You want to see a street gang, eh? Well, I suppose that could be arranged. Of course, it's not at all like it was around here in the 1970s, when we had to deal with so much gang war and open violence," he said.

Sam had all their attention now. Everyone wanted to hear more about what had happened. He told the whole group a little of the South Bronx background he had given those in the van that morning. They listened to the horrors the area suffered.

Youth gangs, he told them, became one of the many problems to stem from the ugliness and destruction of those days. The idea and influence of gangs spread quickly, even to nicer neighborhoods such as the one surrounding Wake-Eden Community Baptist Church.

He told them about one particular time when he had put himself right in the middle of what could have been a violent episode.

It was late one Saturday night, and Sam was in his study at Wake-Eden, preparing his sermon for Sunday. He kept thinking he heard a strange, rumbling kind of noise, but didn't pay much attention until it grew louder and louder. Finally he could tell he was hearing voices. He looked up at the clock and realized that it was after 1:30 A.M. Something was wrong, he knew.

Stepping into the glass-enclosed foyer of the church, Sam saw that his fears were right. The first thing to catch his eye was the dangerous glint of a long silver knife blade in the glow of an overhead street light. Fifteen to 20 teenaged boys were walking past the church, and they were armed with all kinds of city weapons—knives, chains, sticks with razor-blade ends, bottles, even rocks.

It was the sound of their anger that had alerted Sam.

Moving closer to the door, he heard bits and pieces of what they shouted. Threats of "This is our turf" and "I'm going to cut you" told him for certain that this group wanted a confrontation.

As they passed under the street light, he recognized a couple of the boys. There were probably more kids that he knew in the group, maybe even some from his church. The gang was a mix of Italians, Puerto Ricans, and West Indians from the surrounding neighborhood. The fight was going to be about turf, not race.

He started to rush out the door and try to stop them, but he realized that probably wasn't a very smart idea. He didn't know exactly how angry and unreasonable they were. Instead he hurriedly climbed into his big maroon Buick and circled the block. Cutting right in front of the boys he stopped the car about 50 feet ahead of them, just before they met the other gang.

Calling out to the ones he knew, Sam quickly identified himself. Many of them knew him and, he hoped, respected him enough to stop and listen.

"Guys, you don't want to fight," he was saying, when suddenly police cars started coming from every direction. Other people in the community saw what was happening and called the police. The officers began telling everybody to move along, but Sam knew that if these boys left with nothing settled there would just be another, more dangerous confrontation later. He refused to move, and told the policemen who he was.

The police wanted to have a meeting with the groups the next night at the precinct, but the boys refused. They didn't trust the police. Some of the black kids believed the Italian policemen would be hard on them and let the Italians go free. Sam stepped in and suggested they hold the meeting at the church. The police refused, but the kids all shouted, "Yeah, we want to have the meeting at the church!" They trusted Sam to be fair.

The next day he canceled a scheduled trip to Ohio, and prepared for that night's meeting. He asked that only one police car be visible, so that the boys would come. The police agreed to his request, but hid other cars all around the church.

About 80 boys showed up for the meeting. Sam met them at the door.

"There's only one request that I'm making. If you have a gun, knife, switchblade, whatever you have—take it out. Put it away and then come back." About 20 of them left.

Sam stopped talking to sip his tea, and he just looked at the missionaries.

"So then what happened?" two of them said at the same time.

"They came to an understanding of sorts," he said. The meeting started out in chaos, but many of the kids had a chance to express their frustrations. Finally, Sam suggested that both groups select leaders to meet with him and the police captain. With just these few in the other room, they found that neither group really wanted to fight, and that both would be willing to communicate. They set rules about invading each other's turfs, and even agreed to organize basketball teams to play each other.

"That is so cool!" said the girl who wanted to see a gang.

"Well, I don't know if you'd call it cool or not," Sam said.

He had had more than his fill of the violent fraternity of street gangs. Two boys in his church had been gang members, he told the missionaries. They sometimes even wore their jackets with the gang's symbol on the back.

The day one of them turned 15, a member of another gang went to his house and stabbed him. The boy died right there.

Sam conducted his funeral, and he knew how he handled the other gang members would be important.

He was prepared when he saw them begin to file through the door. Even though many of the boys were barely more than children, the group carried a definite air of an ominous secret society. He could almost see the invisible bonds of misplaced honor and violent peer pressure that forced them to keep on playing their deadly games. They all wore black leather jackets bearing the same symbol Sam had seen on the one worn by the boy who had died. Each one walked slowly up to the casket, leaned down and kissed his dead "brother." Their faces were solemn, expressionless masks. Sam stood there watching their empty ritual, but didn't hurry them in any way. Afterwards, as he talked with one of the leaders, the boy invited him to come to a private meeting. He said he wanted Sam to see something.

"And that was how I happened to see for myself how gang members discipline each other," he told the missionaries. "It's pretty rough, pretty rough."

"What do you mean? What do they do?" everyone wanted to know.

He said several times that it was just something he never wanted to see again, or that they would ever want to see. Finally he told them.

In this kind of secret society, he said, when a member divulges some of the secrets, the discipline could be harsh enough to "get rid" of the person. What he saw one night in the darkened basement of a house was a lesser degree of gang discipline.

"Do you know what it is to beat someone with a wet

towel? Do you know what it is to chop off someone's finger with a knife?'' he asked the missionaries. They had heard enough.

"So, gangs are, well, they are not a simple thing anymore. It's not just a fistfight anymore. It's chains and guns and brutalizing. It's killing.''

One of the girls asked Sam if he ever told the gang members about Jesus. He didn't try to explain to her that everything he had done, everything they had just been hearing about, was his way of building relationships with those boys so that he could offer them the hope of Jesus. His actions more than his words said to them, ''I understand your feelings, but God's way is better than the way you have chosen.''

Knowing that he respected them as people made it more likely that the gang members would respect him enough to listen. As with so many other ministries in the city, establishing trust and consistency were the keys to dealing with people such as the gang members he had described. The missionaries, like most Christians confronted with the complexities of witnessing in the city, would soon understand that telling someone about Jesus often had to be surrounded by a whole framework of carefully designed credibility.

"Do you know a neighborhood guy named Don?'' one of the girls asked.

"Yeah,'' one of the boys broke in, "we were talking to him on the street. He knew a lot about the church and stuff.''

"But then he told us all about where we could go to get some crack,'' another of the girls said.

This type of thing was one of the subjects Sam wanted to discuss with the missionaries.

"You are innocent, I guess. I don't know. But I hope you're not naive,'' he said. He did not want to see them get hurt or discouraged, so he warned them to beware of their "sympathetic suburban mind-set."

He told them about a former summer missionary from Texas named Ken who learned this lesson the hard way. He too had met a boy on the street who was on drugs. Sam had known the boy for a long time. One night Ken brought him to the pastor's house. The boy was as high as a kite, but Ken insisted that they give him some coffee, straighten him up, and talk to him about the Lord.

Sam took Ken aside and explained that he knew this boy, and he was not going to sober up in one night.

"Ken, I hate to say this, but that guy is kind of a rock," Sam had said. "He's not going to become sober just because you bring him for coffee."

Ken insisted, so Lola prepared breakfast and coffee for the boy. The missionary witnessed to him, and believed that he accepted Christ. After the boy left, Ken told Sam that he had been too hard on him, that he had been unfair. "I just said, 'All right, Ken. That's OK. Tough love sometimes works.' "

Two days later Ken saw the boy on the street again, in worse shape than he was the night he came for coffee and breakfast and accepted the Lord. He went to Sam, hurt and disappointed.

"So you learn by experience that you cannot win everybody. You cannot help everybody. Some people don't want your help. You just do the best you can," he told the missionaries. "Don't ever believe that you're going to save everybody in the Bronx before you go back home. It's humanly impossible."

While remaining realistic in their expectations, they should also remember that they did have good news to share with everybody, he said.

"We ought to do that, but we should always remember that as many as receive Him, to them He gives the power to become. Everybody's not going to respond, but it's not our job to worry about that.''

He told the missionaries that their job was like the parable about sowing the seed on different grounds. Some of the seed fell on ground that was stony, some among thorns. But the important lesson for them to learn, he said, was what happened to the seed that fell on good ground. Even there, some seed produced 40-, some 60-, and some 100-fold.

"So even on the good ground, there is a kind of proportion. Some will never make a total commitment, and some will. Then some will always be six of one, half a dozen of the other," he said.

The other thing to notice about the parable, he told them, was how it directed them to deal with the problems that would spring up in their ministry.

"The Lord said another guy went out and saw where he had been sowing, and it looked so good. But somebody else came along and threw some other kind of seed amongst his, and he got mad. He decided to go and pull out the bad ones.

"And the Lord said, 'Forget it. Let them stay there. Let me do the weeding out,' '' Sam said.

They should be very careful of their criticisms, he told them, especially of each other. If a brother is overtaken by a fault, speak the truth in love, he reminded them, quoting from Galatians 6.

"Oh, we're ready to handle things like that. We're a family," one of the boys said.

"Well, I hope so. But remember, it takes a lot more than just living in the same house for a week to become a family," Sam responded.

He reminded them that the daily grind of meeting schedules and doing their jobs would soon set in.

"You may get home in the evening hungry and tired,

and there's no one home. The person who was supposed to cook did not cook. You could get mad and decide not to talk to him the rest of the day. These are the kinds of things you'll have to work out in your mind as you start to gel the family,'' he said. It was essential that they be open with each other.

What would destroy them more than anything else, he said, would be to fail in keeping an open communication with the Lord.

"You will think that you are mad with each other, when all the time the Devil will be playing you against you, and you against you," he said, pointing out different members of the group.

"And you'll think that you're wrestling against flesh and blood, when really you're not wrestling against flesh and blood, but principalities and powers that you don't even see. They are in the air. So you're going to have to make sure that your connection with the Lord is such that, well, you know, it's intact.''

Finally, he reminded them of the importance of their role as summer missionaries. While he expected them to be themselves as young people, not "supersaints," he also expected them to always be aware that they were God's representatives. Even in situations that might really tempt them into human reactions, they were to always remember who they were and why they were there.

Again he reminded them to pray. Pray individually, pray as a group, pray in smaller groups. Just be sure to form that bond, he stressed. If they did not get anything else out of their summer as missionaries in the Bronx, Sam wanted them to have the experience of working and living together successfully. He knew that if they stayed in open communication with the Lord and with each other, they could leave having built lifelong friendships.

Sam finished talking. All the laughing and joking had stopped.

"So, you get so pious all of a sudden now. I can say anything now because you all are a captive audience. You'll agree with anything," he said with a wink.

He quickly explained how they would get the money they needed for groceries, their expected duties, and their relationships with assigned supervisors. The meeting was almost over. It was after midnight. Sam was about to wrap things up with a closing prayer when he glanced over his shoulder and noticed Stephen sitting at the table. He had already introduced Kim to the missionaries when she had walked through the dining room earlier. This would be a good time, he thought, to include Stephen.

What he failed to notice was that Stephen had picked up a large sandwich, and was about to take a bite. Just then he said, "Stephen, come and meet these young people."

After just a moment's hesitation, Stephen put his sandwich down and walked over to the group. He listened politely to the names and the small talk. In a few minutes Sam had everyone stand and hold hands. He asked Stephen to say their closing prayer. His son reached out, took the hands of the two girls standing closest to him, and prayed a beautiful prayer on behalf of the missionaries.

The missionaries had been gone for just a few minutes when Lola came upstairs from the basement, where she had been studying for one of her nursing classes. Sam stood in the kitchen scooping ice cream into a bowl.

"How was your meeting?" she asked, rubbing her eyes.

"Oh, it was fine. They're going to be a good group," he said.

"Well, I'm glad to hear that, Sam. Listen, let's go on to bed. I am so tired."

He was already putting ice cream into another bowl for her.

"OK, in a minute. First sit down and have some ice cream with me," he said, handing Lola a bowl and pulling her by the other hand to the couch.

At almost one o'clock in the morning, and with an early class facing her, the last thing Lola wanted to do was stay up and eat ice cream. But she took the bowl and sat down anyway. It had been such a hectic week, she and Sam had hardly seen each other. Losing a few more minutes of sleep wouldn't make that much difference, she decided.

As they sat together eating ice cream and talking about the events of their day, both of them began to forget about the time. Before they knew it they were laughing about something said over dinner.

"That reminds me. You were interrupted right in the middle of a very interesting story about how you stalked and captured me," Lola said.

"What are you talking about? That was no story, it was the truth!" he exclaimed.

"Yes, I know, it was all a part of your master plan. Right, Sam?" she teased, leaning forward to set her empty bowl on the coffee table. She turned around to see a look on her husband's face that changed the playful nature of their conversation.

"No, Lols," he said softly, "even I could not have designed such a grand scheme as having a woman like you for my wife. Surely that was an act of God."

Chapter 7

Sam didn't have any idea what lay in store for him the day his plane landed in Chicago and he first stepped out into bitter cold January air. He didn't know he had set his feet on a path that would eventually lead him to a permanent life in America and a ministry in the Bronx, so different were God's plans from his own.

Like most people reaching the brink of God's purpose for their lives, he didn't recognize the significance of the moment when it came. The realities of a freezing Chicago winter hit Sam harder than any symbolism about entering a new world or starting his life's journey. That too could have just been part of God's plan; because had he known what was ahead, he might not have been able to believe or accept it.

A vague feeling of homesickness tinged Sam's excitement as he settled into his new apartment. The best thing to do, he decided, was to find Emmaus Bible School. A scholarship from this school brought him to the United States to study for the ministry.

He knew the school was in an area called Oak Park, so he decided to take the subway as far as he could, and then find a taxi to carry him to the school. He began trying to find a taxi as soon as he left the subway station. A few went by before he flagged one successfully. Sam climbed into the backseat, gave the driver the address and then leaned back to enjoy the ride. He was looking forward to seeing some of this part of the city.

The driver turned around and looked at him for a minute.

"Where'd you wanna go?"

Sam told him the address again, and smiled.

"Where you from?" the driver asked.

Maybe this gentleman can't understand me because of my accent, Sam thought. He told him he was from Jamaica, and reached out to shake his hand.

"Well, listen," said the driver, "where you're wanting to go is only a half a block from here."

So much for looking like he knew what he was doing.

Sam got out and walked the half block to his school. This wouldn't be the last time he felt foolish as he tried to become accustomed to his new world.

Coming to school in the United States turned out to be more of an adjustment than Sam had anticipated. For one thing, he missed Jamaica. He missed the island itself, with its familiarity, its beauty, and especially its warmth. It would have been hard to find a greater contrast to the Caribbean than Chicago, Illinois, in winter.

Sam found the idea of cold sunshine so foreign that sometimes he had to laugh at his own reactions. The first few times he looked out his window that winter and saw the sun, he went outside without a coat or hat, forgetting it could actually be cold on such a beautiful day. It would be years before he got used to wearing the heavy boots and coats essential for winter survival in Chicago, and later New York. But he would never learn to like this part of American life.

Even more than Sam missed the climate, he missed his

family and friends. At age 28 he had lived away from his parents' home for a long time. But close connections with his large family were still strong, and he missed them terribly. A strange feeling of isolation intensified his loneliness for them. He was accustomed to being a leader in his big circle of friends. But there were only two other students from Jamaica at Emmaus, and he had not known them before they met at school.

Sam accepted all these feelings as normal reactions to new and unfamiliar experiences. He could deal with the expected. But one new experience brought up feelings and reactions he didn't quite know how to handle.

For the first time in his life, Sam felt the sting of an ignorant injustice called prejudice.

In the past he had seen some blacks in Jamaica vie for position based on the degree of lightness or darkness to their skin. He considered that kind of thinking ignorant. Only one word, he decided, could begin to describe such an attitude. *Stupid.* To believe a person's worth could be judged on the color of his skin was one of the most stupid assumptions Sam had ever encountered.

And now for the first time that attitude was being directed toward him. He would never forget his amazement the day he went into a barber shop for a haircut, only to be turned down because he was black. The whole basis for the barber's discrimination was so ridiculous to Sam that he almost laughed in the man's face.

This was the kind of experience with prejudice that American blacks had long endured, and often even accepted. But Sam could not accept it, and the anger and bitterness that began to stir inside him did not fit into his theology. He tried to ignore it by telling himself those experiences were amusing. That wasn't true, though, and he knew it. The more he learned about racism, the less *amusing* he could pretend it to be. That word could never accurately describe something so wrong.

When school began he found himself faced with more disappointment and frustration. He knew there would be differences between his Baptist background and the strict Plymouth Brethren teachings, but felt that their strong emphasis on Bible study would provide enough common ground. It didn't.

Sam's personal view of the clergy—what it meant to be a pastor—constantly clashed with what was being taught in his classes. Even more troubling was an attitude he sensed from the Brethren that he wasn't really quite a Christian.

Then the ugly issue of racism confronted Sam again, this time through one of his evangelism classes. When the academic studies had been completed and it was time to go out into the surrounding neighborhoods for door-to-door witnessing, he and three other black students were not allowed to participate. Instead, they were assigned to do prison ministry at a local jail.

Sam could not deal with the hypocrisy of this situation. Years later he looked back and saw how God used what happened in that class to his advantage. The experience of ministering in the jails proved to be much more useful to him than the traditional visitation would have been. But he couldn't see that at the time. He was greatly troubled by the implications of a Christian school, the school where he was studying for the ministry, making those kinds of decisions.

Sam's background determined to a great extent his reaction to encounters with racism. His typically Jamaican sense of pride and dignity did not depend on how someone else viewed or treated him. His self-image came from within. So while prejudice could do many things to hurt him, it could never change the way he saw Sam Simpson.

Still, he grappled with the anger and resentment that

naturally comes to a young man who suddenly finds himself experiencing the unfairness of racism. He began to develop an unusual personal struggle as he dealt with the problem of prejudice. Instead of feeling put down or inferior, his response was to actually feel superior to the racist.

Because he saw their actions as totally ignorant, he struggled not to think himself better than the white barber who refused to cut his hair, or a white society that accepted or rejected a Christian witness on the basis of color. But as a Christian, Sam knew he would be just as wrong as they were to think in those terms. God made them all, and He loved them all equally.

Those first months in the United States were some of the most unhappy and discouraging in Sam's life. He would go to his room and sing, pray, cry, sleep, worry—whatever he could think of to help face battles within and battles without.

The worst of the realities he struggled to accept was a growing realization that he did not want to continue his studies with the Brethren. This was not the place where he could learn to be the kind of minister he wanted to be.

The end of the year found him so confused that he even doubted his call to enter the ministry. But the idea of going back to Jamaica a failure, with nothing to show for his efforts, was too frightening for Sam to accept. He just couldn't do it.

Eventually he decided to forget about preaching for a while. Instead, he went to New York City, where he could regroup and draw support from friends and family who had moved there from Jamaica.

When he enrolled in the New York Institute of Photography, Sam felt a little relieved about his future. Even if he hadn't become a preacher, he could at least go back to Jamaica as a professional photographer. That was something. It was very important to him to have accomplished something.

One Sunday he decided to visit Calvary Baptist Church. He had heard their radio broadcasts many times in Jamaica, and enjoyed the services. The pastor there had a Brethren background, and he and Sam talked about all the frustrations he experienced in Chicago. He knew the pastor really understood as no one else why he was so confused about his future in the ministry. The more they talked, the more Sam felt his desire to preach beginning to return.

A short time later the pastor told him about a school in New Jersey called Northeastern Bible College. With his encouragement, Sam decided to enroll as a full-time student. He knew then his instincts had been right, that God had in fact called him to preach. With a renewed commitment and dedication, he eagerly plunged into his studies. Where everything felt wrong in Chicago, everything felt suddenly right in New York. He knew he was where God wanted him to be.

With Sam finally in the right place, God's plans quickly began to unfold. Looking back, he knows it was no coincidence that led a fellow Jamaican named David Morgan to preach at Calvary Baptist one Sunday night. Interested in meeting anyone from home, Sam introduced himself after the service.

They talked for a long time. He left that night intrigued by Morgan's stories about his adventures in pastoring a small Southern Baptist congregation struggling to establish the First Baptist Church of Brooklyn. He was curious to meet the kinds of people David Morgan described. A few weeks later he looked up the address Morgan had given him and decided to visit the church.

When Sam got to the address, he looked up at the building in front of him, up and down the street, back at the address, and then again up at the building bearing the correct number. He had the right address. Shrugging his shoulders, Sam went inside and discovered that, yes, the First Baptist Church of Brooklyn did in fact meet upstairs in the YMCA.

Throughout the years to come, Sam would learn that in the city a church doesn't necessarily have to look like a church—not on the outside anyway. Meeting space is accepted anywhere the congregation can find it. Real estate is often too expensive and rents too high, particularly for new and usually small fellowships, to have their own buildings.

A city congregation must be adaptable, especially in its beginning. God can locate His church in the living room of a member's apartment as well as a great cathedral, if that is His plan.

As soon as Sam entered the room where he had been directed, he lost all doubt that he was in the right place. This was definitely church. Most of the people, many of them Jamaican, were around his age. He could easily feel a part of their love for each other and excitement about their purpose. Sam joined the fellowship within a few weeks. But he did more than just find a church home. He officially became a Southern Baptist.

Working with other church members to reach out into the Brooklyn community, Sam began to make discoveries and form attitudes that would have direct bearing on the course of his own ministry.

In the summer of 1962 some Southern Baptist summer missionaries came to help them survey more than 1,000 homes and apartments for the church. Sam was shocked by what he saw.

Until that time he hadn't really known that such poverty existed in a country like the United States. He could not understand how New York City could accept being the home of such abject human misery in the midst of unparalleled wealth and power.

The apathetic attitudes many of the poor adopted about their own lives also upset him. As he went into home after home that was dirty and unkept, as he saw grown men sitting all day on sidewalks, and mothers accepting the same miserable fate for their children, Sam became more and more convicted. Someone had to show these people how God could become more operative in their lives. That was surely their only hope.

Although discovering those hard realities was one of the most emotionally draining experiences of his life, the summer of 1962 proved to be an exciting time of personal growth for him. A deep desire for the people of New York to know God was born in Sam that summer.

The challenge to become a preacher there, to replace the carelessness he had found with morality, to speak out against the injustices that existed, to fight for something as basic as decent housing for those who couldn't fight for themselves—these were the dreams God was writing on his heart. The impressions of those days would in many ways direct the rest of his ministry.

As he began to define his spiritual purpose, the pieces of Sam's personal life also began to come together, like the day he talked to a friend from Jamaica.

"Do you remember my cousin, Lola Campbell?" the friend asked.

"Lola Campbell. Hmm." Sam sat there for a moment, biting his bottom lip as if in thought.

"Oh yes, yes, I believe I do remember her. Miss Lola Campbell. She lived with your family for a time, did she not?" he said.

Yes, he certainly did remember Miss Lola Campbell, much better than he let on. Sam remembered her from the first moment he had seen her and wanted to have her for his wife. He went to great lengths to meet her, and then work his way into a friendship with her cousin. At every opportunity he could manage he saw her and spoke to her.

But Lola hadn't seen in Sam the same possibilities that he saw in her. "What a nice boy," she thought. He was nothing more than a friend, an acquaintance, to her.

Sensing her feelings, he adopted a strategy of patience. He was still waiting for the right moment to make his move when circumstances had separated them and he left Jamaica to study in the United States.

It was a pleasant surprise to hear she had come to New York to pursue a business degree, and now worked at the United Nations.

"Well, perhaps I'll call her, just to chat about home and old friends," Sam said. "Do you have her telephone number?"

Lola's cousin told Sam he did indeed have her number. He didn't tell him that just that week, when he had told Lola Sam lived in New York, she asked for his number.

The day after Sam's conversation with the cousin, Lola's telephone rang.

"Hello, Miss Campbell, this is Sam Simpson."

They talked for a long time about family and friends and homesickness and many other things linking them to a common background. Finally, Sam asked if he might come to visit her. She said that would be nice. A nice friendly visit.

To date Lola he would have to drive all the way from his aunt's house in Brooklyn, where he lived, to her aunt's house in the Bronx, where she lived. He never considered the inconvenience, and hoped to make the trip many times in the weeks to come.

Lola looked forward to seeing Sam, remembering him as a nice boy from home. But when the doorbell rang and she opened the door, she didn't quite recognize the man standing there smiling at her.

There had been something different about him when they talked on the phone, but she couldn't quite put her finger on it. Seeing him now she realized he was older, somehow more mature. Her attitude about their date changed immediately.

"Ah, this is good husband material," she thought to herself as she asked him in.

They spent the evening laughing and talking, catching up on each other's lives. By the time they went outside for a walk, Sam decided he had been patient long enough. It was time to test the waters. A bit nervously, he reached out and took her hand. She didn't pull it away. They walked on. He gave her hand a little squeeze. She squeezed back.

"This is not Jamaica anymore. This is America!" Sam thought to himself, pleased with the turn the evening had taken.

They began seeing each other regularly. One day he asked if she would like to go with him to church. She agreed, and the next Sunday he drove from Brooklyn out to the Bronx to get her, then back to Brooklyn for church.

Sam was always joking, and when he parked the car and then directed her to the YMCA building, Lola stopped outside and shook her head.

"I don't believe you. You told me you were taking me to church!" she said.

The childhood teachings of a formal Anglican background tied her idea of church closely to the building where it was located. She was much more shocked than Sam had been to discover a church housed in the YMCA. But, like him, she quickly fell in love with the young people who met in that upstairs room. Her social life with Sam soon began to revolve around this church.

Although she was always eager to be there, Sam knew exactly why Lola came to church. She came for the fun and fellowship, nothing more. They had not discussed it directly, but he knew she had no intentions of embracing his dedication. Something must have happened, he knew, to make her so indifferent to the messages she heard service after service. He knew his plans for the ministry and his plans for marriage must be compatible. So as their relationship grew more serious, he spent much time in prayer about Lola and the future.

The sermons she heard about being born again and having a personal relationship with God were not new to Lola. She knew the right words well enough to have preached them herself. Many, many times as a child she attended evangelical meetings with relatives or friends. She memorized all the hows and whys of salvation.

But at age 13, when she was about to be confirmed in the Anglican church, she knew there must be something more. The day before her confirmation, she asked the rector to explain exactly what all that talk about being born again and saved really meant.

He became annoyed. That question did not fit into the prescribed teachings of the church. He refused to answer. She was confirmed the next day, more confused than ever about religion and all its implications.

During the next few years, she continued to go to different evangelical meetings. At one of them she became very convicted, and went to the altar for counseling. The gospel speaking to her heart was being filtered through a lifetime of teachings about the right words, the wrong words, the right church, the wrong church.

Still confused, but wanting to respond, she asked the evangelist, "What is the right church?"

Like the rector years before, he too became annoyed.

"I preach Jesus!" he said, and stalked away.

Lola was left hurt, embarrassed, more confused than ever, and still unsaved. For all her seeking, no one had been willing to help her. She decided right then she was through with religion. As soon as she left home to live on her own, going to church became a thing of her past. But that began to change when Sam introduced her to the social life of Brooklyn's First Baptist Church.

What she didn't realize was that Sam was patiently plotting to break down her indifference. As he prayed and exposed her to the word of God, she began to lose her defenses.

Finally, one Saturday night she was alone at home, cleaning the house. As she stood there with a dust cloth in her hand, it seemed as if the room suddenly became alive around her. The aliveness was like a light. And then she heard a voice saying, "I'm inviting you to come to Me."

Whether the voice was in her mind or in the room she did not know. But she knew it was God asking her to come to him.

"OK, God," she heard herself saying.

That was it. That was all she said. And in that instant her life completely changed. Finally, she understood that finding the right words didn't matter because God knew rightness of heart when He heard it. The years of searching and confusion were gone. A love and freedom that Lola had never before experienced replaced her indifference.

Riding the subway to Brooklyn the next day, she could hardly wait to get to church. Sam didn't know about what had happened. When the invitation came, the reality of her situation overwhelmed her. On her way down the aisle, tears began to flow. She became conscious of her sin and the need to confess. As she repented and prayed, Lola experienced the cleansing of Jesus Christ, and finally knew what it really meant to be saved.

She and Sam spent most of that afternoon in his aunt's living room, praying and talking. God confirmed many things for him, and in just a few weeks he asked Lola to be his wife.

She happily said yes and they began to make their plans. One day as they prayed together again, the awesome responsibility of what might be in store became very clear to her. She was certain God had great plans for Sam, and she wanted to be just as certain she fit into those plans. Sam was moved by the simple honesty with which his future wife told God the desires of her heart.

"God, I love this man. I want to marry him. But I don't want to get in his way. If you see that I shouldn't marry him, it's OK by me. And if you see that I should, that's OK too."

God's answer was to give Lola the same assurance He had given Sam.

Their next hurdle, not nearly so spiritual, was to decide on a wedding date. Sam wanted July of that year, 1963. Marrying then would give them two months before his school term started in September. The romance of driving from Brooklyn to the Bronx had faded long ago, and he had no desire to add to that another drive to college in New Jersey every day. His bride, however, said absolutely not. There was no way they could possibly plan a decent wedding in that short amount of time. He was crazy to think they could. They would just have to wait.

That July Sam married Lola and settled the debate.

They planned a quiet honeymoon at a New York mountain resort. Driving away from the wedding reception they began to talk about their life together and dream about the future as newlyweds often do. Caught up in their conversation and each other, they didn't notice how long they drove.

But as the surroundings became more and more deserted, and the mountain road more and more winding, they began to pay attention. Sam had followed the directions exactly, he thought, but the further they drove, the less likely it looked that they were approaching any kind of mountain resort. It was so dark and the road so bad that the only safe speed was practically zero. Finally, way past midnight, they agreed they were hopelessly lost. There didn't appear to be anything to do but park the car and wait for daylight.

In the morning, just around the next bend, they found their honeymoon resort.

The following year was a busy one for the newlyweds. They made their home in Brooklyn, so Sam still drove to New Jersey every day to attend classes. He served as a deacon and taught a Sunday School class at First Baptist Brooklyn, which by that time had grown so fast that it had moved into a "proper" building. In September the church ordained Sam to the ministry.

One day not long after Sam's ordination Lola woke up feeling so sick she could hardly get out of bed. The nausea got worse instead of better, and lasted for the next nine months. With every one of her children, Lola was sick before she knew she was pregnant.

As usual, Sam handled all the responsibilities and pressures of his life underneath a characteristically calm, cool exterior. He might have been meeting himself coming and going as he juggled a hectic schedule while taking care of a pregnant wife. But no one knew when he was stressed or tired. No one, not even Lola, would ever guess how he suffered watching her struggle through those long months of sickness. Already, his wife had become so much a part of him that when she suffered, so did he.

The following summer their first daughter, Erica, was born. The baby had no choice but to be flexible and easygoing like her father. She entered their lives just as

Sam was preparing to launch his ministry.

Committed to his vision of changing lives in New York City, he quickly agreed when David Morgan and other state Southern Baptist leaders asked him to start a church in Manhattan. But that wasn't the location God had in mind, and after several unsuccessful attempts they discontinued their efforts.

He and Lola began looking for an apartment in the Bronx where many of their friends lived. One of those friends, who had become particularly close to Lola, attended First Baptist Brooklyn. Her Christian commitment greatly deepened there. Hearing about their plans to live in the Bronx, she suggested they start a Bible study in her apartment.

When Sam seized this second opportunity to start a church, the Home Mission Board appointed him as an associate missionary. He, Lola, Erica, the woman who owned the apartment, three people from First Baptist Brooklyn, three Christians Sam had known in Jamaica, and one man from a Brethren church became the nucleus of a congregation that would eventually grow into Bronx Baptist Church.

Sam immediately began looking for a building. In August 1964 he discovered a small two-story structure for sale in the South Bronx. More than 100 years old, it had most recently been used as a Jewish synagogue. The Home Mission Board agreed with his choice of location, and purchased the building on Honeywell Avenue.

The arrangement was for the church to meet downstairs, while Sam, Lola, and Erica lived upstairs. Lola would never forget the first time she left work and went to their new home.

Ever since coming to New York she had worked and lived only in the nicer areas. Her aunt's house in the Bronx had been on a beautiful tree-lined street. She left there every day to go to the United Nations in Manhattan. When she and Sam married they lived overlooking the river in a very good part of Brooklyn. She had never lived in an apartment house or a poor area of the city.

Lola began to realize just how fortunate she had been the minute she got off the subway and began walking toward her new home on Honeywell Avenue. It was the day after a citywide garbage strike, and in an act of defiance people lined both sides of the street with open garbage cans from the huge apartment buildings. For three blocks Lola walked surrounded by garbage, becoming more shocked and horrified with each step.

In addition to the garbage, tall apartment houses loomed over her, grim and dirty looking. Too many people loitered on the streets, their faces reflections of either anger or indifference. It was almost as if a cloud hung over the entire area. By the time she got home Lola was reeling at the thought of making her home in such a place.

She had never imagined that in a city like New York people lived under these conditions. Her awakening was similar to the one Sam experienced the summer he went into the poor areas of Brooklyn.

That night as she thought about what she and her husband had committed themselves to do, Lola prayed earnestly about her reaction. She knew she would be no good to Sam if she hated being where God placed them.

Finally, she was able to say, "Well, this is God's work." And then began what she would call one of the greatest miracles of her life. Lola started seeing beauty in the people and the neighborhood around her. The disgust and repulsion she first experienced were completely erased.

"God just took it," she would tell people for years to come.

Friends from the United Nations heard her talk about the church, and agreed to come.

"This is what you've been talking about?" they would say in disbelief when they visited for the first time.

Her descriptions didn't match up to the surroundings they saw. But they did to Lola. Without her attitude, Sam knew he wouldn't have been able to face his task with the same enthusiasm.

One week after the 16-member congregation moved into what they called the Honeywell Chapel, their membership had almost doubled. Steady growth began to take place. Sam and Lola worked hard to make themselves a part of the community. They participated in the YWCA. Sam became involved in the Community Planning Board. The church held street meetings. They did everything they could think of to open themselves to the needs around them.

The chapel developed much the same spirit as First Baptist Brooklyn. The people who came were mostly young, struggling to make ends meet as they pursued educations and established homes. They easily developed a feeling of camaraderie, which was strengthened by the generous hospitality of the young pastor and his wife.

Lola would always remember the warmth and welcome she received from David Morgan and his wife. Mrs. Morgan in particular went out of her way to enhance the family atmosphere of the church. Thrown into a similar role, Lola couldn't think of any better model to follow than hers.

So their home became a constant open house. Every Sunday at least 10 or 12 people would follow the welcoming aromas of lunch cooking upstairs to the pastor's dining room. Lola's table would be spread with the island dishes she loved to serve.

Those meals almost always featured her Jamaican specialty—a roast that made its own spicy gravy after it had been cored and stuffed with garlic, black pepper, salt, and onions, and then left to soak overnight. The secret of a Jamaican roast, Lola told many visitors, was in the gravy.

There would also be fried chicken, rice and beans cooked in coconut juice (or rice and peas, as it was known to the Jamaicans), fried plantains, and always a long, cold drink of fruit juices with lots of ice.

After the meal they would sit and talk for hours. God used these times of fellowship to form the bonds they would need in order to meet the challenges at hand.

The many groups of Southern Baptist volunteers Sam was beginning to bring to the Bronx were also received into his home openly. They often made their headquarters there. A pile of sleeping bags stashed in the corner was a common sight in their living room. And Lola never knew who might be coming to spend a night or a week or a month in the extra bedroom.

One Thanksgiving 20 students from New Orleans Baptist Theological Seminary came to work with the church during their holiday break. Lola took away any fears of sacrificing their Thanksgiving to serve God. All of them joined the Simpsons that day for a meal they would never forget.

"You don't live above a church. You have a church in your house!" a friend once told Sam and Lola.

But that was the way they wanted it, and that whole time held a special aura for them. Sam knew he was being led by God, and his entire ministry took on a feeling of absolute excitement. They were so committed to the ministry that nothing in their lives seemed more important.

In less than two years, the chapel was constituted as Bronx Baptist Church. Almost 100 people joined their small fellowship, and the building was past holding the growing congregation.

Those first few had had a vision of building a church that would outgrow Cecelia Robinson's living room and then the little chapel on Honeywell Avenue. They prayed and planned and hoped for the day an even larger building would have to be found. But when the time actually came, they looked around with some nostalgia.

Like Lola, they could no longer see the bad. Because God had already been so good, Sam knew that it would take an extra measure of His grace to help them continue to look forward instead of back.

Chapter 8

Being a leader comes naturally to Sam. Throughout almost 30 years of ministry, just doing his job has placed him in greater and greater positions of responsibility. Even as an eager young preacher struggling to establish his first church, he began building bridges that would help him reach his goals.

He doesn't know the meaning of the word *no* when it comes to being obedient in carrying out God's plans. He doesn't bother with logic. If he wants something badly enough, he will somehow find a way to get it. Lola often says reason is a thing that has never stood in the way of her husband's "illogical Jamaican" tenacity. But finding a way, even when there isn't one, is the only option Sam sees on his missions field.

It took several years to find the building that Bronx Baptist Church now occupies. What many other people called failures in the search, he chose to view as redirections.

Conditions became more and more crowded at Honeywell Avenue, and Sam grew certain that God was leading them to a bigger building and larger ministries. His contacts all over the Bronx helped him look for the right place, but nothing ever seemed to work out. There was plenty of opportunity to become discouraged, especially when one particularly innovative solution offered by the Twin Parks Association failed.

Sam wanted to rent "space" in one of the newly refurbished high-rise apartment buildings. The plan was to locate the church on the bottom floor, and offices in the space between the church and apartments above. He saw it as an ideal location, holding countless opportunities for ministry. The only obstacle standing in their way was $145,000 for the church portion. They couldn't manage to get the money, and the deal fell through.

But Sam refused to let himself or his congregation dwell on the disappointment. He worked to redirect their efforts and keep their greater goals in perspective.

Then one day a friend called. Sam had asked several people to be on the lookout for an available building. His friend found two possibilities. Both were located on the same corner, about three blocks from the major Bronx business district. Middle- and low-income apartment houses surrounded the buildings.

Sam listened as his friend described both buildings. The smaller one, at $40,000, was the one he recommended Bronx Baptist try to buy. The owner was asking $145,000 for the larger building, a cost previously out of their price range. As his friend continued to talk, Sam was already forming a plan in his mind. He wanted the larger building, a beautiful old brick church with stained glass windows and an auditorium ready to hold 350 people.

After some hard bargaining with the owners, he negotiated the price down to $85,000. This time when Sam turned to the Home Mission Board, they granted the needed funds. Bronx Baptist rejoiced that their search was over. They bought the building and immediately began working to repay the loan. Just 16 years later, they burned that mortgage at the church's 20th anniversary celebration.

Soon after the Bronx Baptist building was purchased, Sam began looking around the middle-class neighborhood where he and Lola had bought a house. An idea kept tugging at the back of his mind, until one day he saw a Lutheran church for sale just a few blocks away. That was all it took for Sam to put his idea into action. Bronx Baptist soon extended its ministry by renting the building and forming a congregation there. But he was never satisfied, and by 1979 they had purchased the church connecting the Wake-Eden house where the summer missionaries stayed.

It was clear very early in his ministry that Sam was going to cause things to happen wherever he went. By 1966 he had received full missionary status from the Home Mission Board, and just six years later became pastor-director of all Southern Baptist work in the Bronx, giving valuable insight to the Board's planning and promotion for the cities.

It was in the pastor-director role that he began to emerge as an important leader for Baptists in New York. Pastor-director was a tough job, combining the responsibilities of pastoring a church with directing new work in surrounding areas. Few people had been successful at making the plan work; it was difficult to concentrate on both church growth and church starting at the same time. It was just too much for one man to do. But God had been preparing Sam for such a job ever since his childhood in Jamaica.

He grew up in a system where one pastor served a whole circuit of churches. The solution he had seen work time and again for pastors in Jamaica was to more actively involve the church laypeople. There was no reason not to try that solution in the United States, he figured, and it worked.

Sam never saw any need for one man to shoulder all the responsibility alone. His natural ability to motivate people and his strong personal commitment to building lay leadership perfectly suited him for the pastor-director role.

While successfully strengthening his churches on the inside, he built outside ties that are essential to effective city ministry. The committed Christian in New York City finds out fast that he can't go it alone. This reality is often a perplexing problem for Southern Baptists, who form a tiny minority in the area.

The Baptist Convention of New York includes all of New York State, northern New Jersey, and western Connecticut. About 25,000 Southern Baptists minister to the 26,000,000 people living within those confines.

In the Metropolitan Association alone, where both Bronx Baptist and Wake-Eden are located, only 150 Southern Baptist churches serve a city of approximately 7.3 million people. They are ministering in a place where almost half the population is foreign born. Language alone separates them from a vast opportunity to witness.

Because of this giant mixture of people in Sam's world, every attempt at ministry is complicated by a wide array of needs. A world-class city presents problems that are multiclass, multicultural, multiracial. And even those problems never prove simple.

Some areas, for example, cannot be categorized as just "black." There may be American blacks, Jamaican blacks, African blacks—all living in the same area, but all with different backgrounds, different problems, different needs. And they all call for a unique approach.

Every one of those very different 7.3 million people find themselves crowded into such a relatively small area that population density alone changes the way they live. From the pace of living to the cost of living, everything is affected.

If Southern Baptists are going to accomplish anything in the face of these facts, Sam knows they must have confidence in their own strength. He is convinced the churches must know what they believe and why, and never compromise those beliefs.

But he also knows that no one can survive in isolation, especially in the city. The church is no exception to that rule. He has learned the importance of tying churches in pioneer areas like New York closely to the Southern Baptist network of support. He has also learned how to reach outside that denominational network to Christians of other backgrounds. There is room enough for all of them. They all need each other.

These beliefs led Sam to become involved in the Council of Churches of the City of New York to the point of being elected president in 1980. With its strength in numbers, the council is able to look more comprehensively at the needs of the entire city. One church or denomination could not begin to make the impact that all of them make together.

Because of its broad scope and influence, the council provides a valuable connection between the secular world and the churches. This connection often results in opportunities for ministry that might not otherwise be open.

For example, one year when the US Department of Energy wanted to allocate $1 million to help poor people in New York have a warmer winter, they turned to the Council of Churches. The council took the oil company penalty money and set up the Winter Heat Crisis Fund. With the assistance of local ministers, they identified the people who most needed help.

Instead of more dollars being blindly doled out to faceless people, a real service was performed. One church alone would never have received that money, but through the council many churches felt a part of the ministry it provided.

And if people were going to be spared a winter of freezing apartments with no heat, Sam was glad they had a reason to give their thanks to God rather than the government.

Opening the Center for the City was something he was especially glad to see happen during his presidency. The center is a place where people with problems ranging from drug abuse to alcoholism to AIDS can go for help.

By involving his churches in efforts such as this center, he helps his members plug into ministry opportunities outside their individual reach. Many of the council's projects are larger versions of the church's own ministries, like feeding the hungry or giving jobs to unemployed teens.

But the benefits of working with the council are measured not just in terms of what his churches are able to give. Because of the influence and recognition afforded to Sam, a Southern Baptist pastor and missionary, the entire denomination is strengthened in the state.

If nothing else, just having fewer people in New York City hear the name *Southern Baptist* and ask, ''What's that?'' makes their job a little easier.

That's why he takes every opportunity to explain the beliefs of his denomination, and expand its limited reputation in New York. Using Southern Baptist preachers, musicians, and laypeople to fill his allotted council-paid radio and television time is more than just providing a ministry. It's also good public relations.

Southern Baptist work in New York is further strengthened when one of its own is seen associating with famous and influential people. Self-image is often more important than public image, particularly if you are small and facing giant obstacles.

Every year the Council of Churches of the City of New

York recognizes a world leader with its prestigious Family of Man award. Some of the recipients selected during Sam's presidency included President Jimmy Carter, Bishop Desmond Tutu, and in 1981, Prime Minister Pierre Trudeau of Canada.

A gala dinner at the Waldorf Astoria ballroom surrounded the award's presentation that year. Among the hundreds of people there were some of New York's most socially elite, along with many members of council churches. As those attending prepared to enjoy the evening, they had no idea of the crisis going on behind the scenes.

Gerald Ford, former President of the United States, was to present the award to Prime Minister Trudeau. But just a few days before the dinner Ford suddenly took ill. He would not be able to make the presentation.

All the publicity surrounding the dinner mentioned his participation. It was too late to get someone of Ford's prominence to fill in. Frantic planners did not want to disappoint the audience, and they especially didn't want to offend the award recipient. Finally, the council's executive director decided to call the prime minister and ask who he would like to have make the presentation.

"Why, I request your president, Rev. Samuel Simpson, to do me the further honor of presenting the award!" Trudeau graciously said.

Everyone was greatly relieved, except possibly Sam, who would be facing an audience expecting to see the former President of the United States.

Just before the award ceremony, a young woman who was an active member of a local Baptist church sang "He's Got the Whole World in His Hands." Everyone in the room seemed to be holding their breath as she finished the most majestic, moving rendition they had ever heard of that familiar old song. It happened that she was also a member of the Metropolitan Opera. The audience was obviously stirred, but no one more so than the prime minister. The moment was heavy with potential. The next words could either enhance the spirit that had been created, or deflate it.

Sam stood to introduce the honoree. Sensing the mood, he decided against the introduction he had jotted down earlier.

Instead he turned to the prime minister and said, "Now, sir, we await your sermon."

Trudeau did not miss the point.

"President Simpson, distinguished guests, I do have a message for this hour," he said, and delivered an address with the power and urgency of a sermon.

Sam had handled the situation deftly. He gave Prime Minister Trudeau the highest moment of the night. He had called out the best from the speaker, and set an attitude of expectation for the listeners.

Seizing a moment is something Sam has a special knack for doing well. His ability to do this often makes a point that words would not have been able to capture.

When the Bronx elected a new borough president, Sam invited him to attend a morning worship service. It turned into more than just another political appearance for the politician when Sam asked if he would come down to the front of the church. He then led the entire congregation to pray for the new president.

By simply calling for prayer, Sam caused every member of his church to think about the importance of their involvement in making their community a better place to live. They had talked time and time again about the changes that needed to be made in the neighborhood and in the city. Here before them stood someone who could either help or hurt those efforts.

As the people reflected on their own responsibilities,

the new borough president left knowing how serious Sam Simpson's churches are about their role in impacting the community.

Sam leads the people of his churches to have a strong commitment to social action, but always based on a ministry of prayer.

A reputation for integrity and wise leadership that transcends racial, cultural, and financial barriers has caused Sam to be consulted many times by borough and city leaders. His influence extends all the way to the office of New York Mayor Ed Koch.

One Saturday afternoon a friend went to Bronx Baptist Church looking for Sam. He knew the pastor usually stopped by there to visit with the people who came for the free meal. The friend was surprised to see a long black limousine parked in front of the church. He later learned the mayor had sent a special envoy to discuss one of his programs with Sam.

"Is the mayor in town today, Sam? I know he always checks with you before leaving," his friend often teased after the incident.

But it is a fact that many people would describe Sam Simpson as the most influential black pastor in New York City.

It was a natural step for the Southern Baptists of New York to elect him to two terms as president of their convention. Denominational service is not a new experience for Sam. Way back at Honeywell he became involved in the Metropolitan Association, where he eventually served as moderator.

Many of his duties as state convention president are what he calls ceremonial in nature. He presides at convention sessions and brings greetings in churches on behalf of New York Baptists. He also helps administer the business of the convention. Appropriately during his presidency Baptists of New York purchased their first headquarters building, and volunteers from Georgia and South Carolina helped renovate the inside of the building.

As a national convention leader, Sam is also in a position to better combat what he considers one of the most serious problems facing the denomination. If Southern Baptists really want to be effective in the years ahead, they must, he believes, change their traditionally held bias against the city. A stronger word for that bias is *prejudice,* and he understands very well the results of such thinking.

The denomination has set out to tell America about Christ. Most Southern Baptists have heard the words *Bold Mission Thrust,* but not enough have realized they'll never accomplish its goals outside the cities. Few of them recognize an inherited belief that somehow God has abandoned the cities and directed His gospel elsewhere.

All too often efforts are poured into telling the message to traditional audiences, while the great masses of people gathered in the cities are left still waiting to hear with only a few Christians to tell them the good news. Many Christians who are genuinely committed to the ideas of Bold Mission Thrust can't really believe that people in the cities are willing to receive the gospel. Too often they see the city only in terms of its evil, ugliness, and sin, Sam knows.

This view is dangerously one-sided for Christians about to enter the next century. It is most dangerous because of the illusion it creates. What people see as completely evil or hopeless they more easily dismiss as unreachable, not worth their effort. And if that happens to Southern Baptists and the cities, the denomination will lose its efforts to win America for Christ, Sam believes. Trends say perhaps eighty percent of the nation's population could be urban in just a little more than ten years—the end of this century. Sam knows this means that if too many fellow Southern Baptists continue to emphasize sharing the gospel in limited rural terms, they will only be heard by two out of ten people. He can't accept a future like that.

Quinn Pugh, the New York convention's executive director, voiced the message Sam has been working to spread to the rest of the denomination for many years.

The Bible repeatedly points Christians to the cities, he says.

"The Bible is a remarkably urban book, not rural as we have so often interpreted it. It was to the cities that God sent the prophets. It was over the city that our Lord wept. It was to the cities and villages that He sent His disciples. It was to the great cities of the first century that the Apostle Paul carried the gospel. It is to the Holy City, the new Jerusalem, that we are pointed in the Revelation.

"How surprising that we have been unwilling to invest our missionary priorities, the resources of personnel and money, in the massive urban areas of America."

Sam's strategy to combat prejudice against the city is similar to the one he uses to fight prejudice against people. With love and patience, he quietly works, one by one, to dispel the fears and myths about his missions field.

His desire to break down barriers of all kinds in sharing the love of Christ has not been limited just to New York, or even the United States. Sam has been active in personally carrying the gospel abroad to Africa, India, and Europe.

In India he saw handfuls of Christians facing a magnitude of human need that even New York City couldn't rival. He later wrote that he would never forget the experience of spending 17 days traveling more than 3,000 miles inside a country where 550 million people live without the saving knowledge of Jesus Christ. Most of those people live in poverty not even conceivable by American standards.

A jumble of images that would continue to haunt Sam

included "buildings whose styles range from ancient to grass thatched to modern. Some people living in palaces, some sleeping in parks. Horns blaring, cows walking the streets and depositing their waste. And so many, many people everywhere."

For eight days he preached in evangelistic tent meetings and conventional Indian worship services. Altogether, 175 people accepted Christ and rededicated their lives. Among them were four Hindu medical students, a great breakthrough for Christians in their area.

Wherever he went, Sam adapted his approach to best meet the needs at hand. In the Indian churches where women worshiped on one side of the room and men another, he too removed his shoes and sat cross-legged on the floor on a straw mat. Whether it was organizing a cricket game with young people after the tent meetings or talking with other passengers on crowded, dust-filled trains, he could not resist an opportunity to meet people at their point of need.

There is no such thing as a vacation from the ministry for Sam. On a bus tour through Europe, he and Lola were looking forward to releasing some of their responsibilities and just being typical American tourists on vacation. But when he stepped inside that bus and saw 21 people captive with no means of escape, the opportunity was too attractive to pass up. After one or two days of general conversation and getting to know the group, he couldn't stand it any longer.

There were 11 or 12 nationalities represented, with religious beliefs that ranged from Roman Catholic to Pentecostal to Muslim to Jewish to none. Careful not to offend anyone, he checked with the tour coordinator, and after getting his OK, offered himself as the bus chaplain.

The passengers agreed, and at the beginning of each day he led a time of prayer for safe travel.

"Even an atheist," he thought, looking down mountainsides at hairpin curves, "is human enough not to resist a little help on roads like this."

Surrounded by the spectacular beauty of European mountains and valleys, it was easy and natural to talk about the glory and majesty of God. Before they knew it, Sam expanded the morning prayertimes to include singing, testimonies, and even a little preaching.

An unusual closeness developed among the strangers on the bus. When Sam was late coming aboard, he would find the passengers asking each other, "Where's the pastor? When is the pastor coming on?"

His availability and willingness to look at people through the eyes of Jesus changed a vacation into a spiritual experience for the people on that bus, and possibly planted seeds that would eventually change their lives.

When his holiday ended and Lola returned to the States, Sam stayed on in England to join a Foreign Mission Board-sponsored partnership missions group that was en route from New York. Three other men from his churches were part of the otherwise all-white group of about 40 Southern Baptist volunteers. They were to spend two weeks working with Baptist churches in the London area.

Although Sam was an experienced preacher and his church members articulate, competent laymen, the white project coordinators had a hard time placing them.

When their assignment came, it was to an inner-city church that was 75 percent black. Sam and the other men trusted God, and set out to share their witness with the people there. For 15 days they visited in homes, met with community groups, talked with young people, encouraged black English Baptist leadership, and preached in church services.

Many of the people Sam met while visiting in the community came to England from Jamaica for their education, and had settled there. He had known some of them when they were young. Renewing these friendships was a surprise for him. And as an added blessing, several of those people joined the church as a result of their contact with Sam.

A member of Bronx Baptist had given Sam the address of her sister, who lived in London, and asked that they try to find an opportunity to speak to her. It turned out she lived very near the church where they were assigned. After several attempts to reach her at home, they learned she was in the hospital. They were unsuccessful at reaching her there. Instead of giving up, one rainy evening they finally found her at home.

As they talked, it became evident her needs were much greater than just hearing a word from her sister. They counseled and prayed with her for several hours, and that night led her to know the Lord. She too became a member of the church they represented.

God blessed their faithfulness, and they saw many lives change as a result of their ministry there. One man came to the service on Sam's last Sunday because it was the nearest church to his house, and it was raining that day. He later wrote this letter:

Dear Sam:

I am writing to thank you and your colleagues for the spiritual upliftment and refreshment of my faith that you gave to me recently (on your visit to Woodgrange Baptist Church) at a time when I needed it most. . . .

My faith was wearing thin and my prayers were dying on my lips. . . . I believe that God guided me that morning because I was reinspired by the messages that you and your colleagues shared . . . and I emerged with my faith restored and fresh hope in my heart. . . .

I now have a faith and trust in God and His working for good in my life that is stronger than ever. Whatever the future holds for me, I don't believe that faith will now ever leave me. . . . My love for God and my trust in Him had been made known to me in a way that I had never been able to fully understand previously.

At the end of the trip, when all the volunteers reassembled for debriefing, the coordinator spoke to Sam about the problems they had encountered in trying to find a place for them to work. He struggled to choose words that would help them all believe race had not been the issue.

Once again seizing the moment, Sam laughed with him and said, "Yes, I realize what a plight you were all confronted with. We prayed for you."

There was no mistaking his point. "But you know what?" he went on to say, "You didn't work it out, and I didn't work it out. The Lord put us where He wanted us to be, and that was one of the most beautiful experiences we have ever had."

There are many things that can interfere with the plans of God if His people fail to walk in His spirit. But if they don't fail, if they are faithful to what He has called them to do, they can be used anywhere.

Chapter 9

Whatever Sam was to become in America would always be determined, to some extent, by what his life had been in Jamaica.

To the outsider looking in, there was little about his childhood that made him suitable for the world he would inhabit as an adult. But almost every day Sam is aware of some small way God used those early years to prepare him for what lay ahead.

Especially today, a muggy Sunday afternoon in New York, he was reminded of the carefree days he spent growing up on his father's farm.

Sam had come to Bronx Baptist to help prepare for the night's street meeting. His churches and missions all hold outdoor evening services during the months of July and August. Today was a particularly hot day, and a relentless sun made setting up sound equipment and metal chairs punishing work. That night's service would be held in the short dead-end street next to the church.

Pulling a white handkerchief out of his pocket and wiping his face, Sam leaned against a parked car to rest. A sound down the street caught his attention. Looking in that direction, he smiled at what he saw. Some children from a nearby apartment building had opened a fire hydrant, and squealed with delight as they took turns jumping in and out of the cool spray.

From where he stood Sam could see their faces. They were oblivious to the rest of the world. The heat of the day was forgotten in their joy of the moment. Envious adults glanced in their direction, secretly wishing they could lose their inhibitions and join the game.

One little boy stood just at the edge of the water's arc, his arms outstretched, his head tilted back as far as it would go. He had closed his eyes against the water hitting him right in the face, but his mouth was open, and he was laughing.

"That's what it feels like to be a child who is lost in play," Sam thought, "happy just to be a part of the world around you."

Something about that little boy reminded him of himself, and for an instant he was eight years old again, running through his father's cornfield with his best friend Hector. Being the son of one of the small community's most respected planters had many advantages. But to a small boy playing hide-and-seek, a tall stand of corn was the best advantage of all.

For the children of New York City, a concrete sidewalk and an open fire hydrant are as happy a playground as that cornfield had been to Sam. The city is as much a part of them as they are of it, and Sam understands that they wouldn't trade their world any more than he, at their age, would have traded his.

Where, Sam often thought, would the thousands of New York children without that safe system of home and community find the support to reach their potential? He was convinced that for many of them, his churches could fill some of the gaps. He couldn't give them the happiness of his childhood, but he could help them find the happiness of theirs.

He grew up believing himself to be the most fortunate boy alive to have been born a child of Luther and Mary Simpson. The love and acceptance he experienced from them freed him to become secure and happy. A close, caring community continually reinforced that positive self-image.

Only Sam's parents influenced his life more than the preachers and church members he knew as a child.

The family enjoyed a prominent place in the community, where both his father and mother were well-known leaders. Being a planter did not mean being poor for Luther Simpson, who was considered financially successful. He raised many typical farm animals, including his own cattle. And in addition to the corn, he grew just about anything he could find space for—coffee, yams, potatoes, peas, bananas. Sam would never lose a taste for the island staples he grew up eating fresh from his father's fields.

Besides being a planter, Luther served the community as district constable. In New York terms, he was the local cop. Years later as Sam served on his local police precinct board, many things he learned from observing his father helped him to be sensitive to both police and community. As he intervened on behalf of boys from dangerous street gangs, he was well aware of the tightrope walked by the city policeman. All too often he doesn't trust the people, and they don't trust him. And he never knows how and when his life might be threatened.

But none of those frightening thoughts had been necessary in the life of a boy whose father served as a community police officer in the 1930s Jamaica of Sam's childhood. What he remembered most was seeing the many people who respected his father's position coming to him for advice or counseling. It was not unusual to see his father and another man sitting outside at the family's barbecue pit or on a corner of the porch talking for hours.

Sometimes they would be discussing a situation faced by many of the poorer people in the area. While a wife sat crying in the kitchen with his mother, Sam's father would be listening to the husband's plans to leave Jamaica in search of farm work in the United States.

As a little boy, he couldn't understand what was going on, and it bothered him a great deal. In the security of his world, he could not imagine why a man would leave his homeland and go to work in another country. Years later, as he faced the ugly realities of poverty in New York City, he recalled those first images of people struggling to hold their lives together.

Church filled a major part of the Simpson family's life. Both parents were active leaders of Gibraltar Baptist Church. Luther served as a deacon. They made Sunday School and worship services the family priority, even though the church was a long way from their house. They traveled the dirt roads in a horse-drawn wagon, unless Sam's uncle happened to come by with his truck.

A family altar served as the center of their home, and prayertime was strictly observed. As Sam formed those earliest habits, there were many times he would rather have been playing marbles or throwing a football than taking that bumpy ride to church or praying with his family.

Sometimes he resented having to conform to those practices, but his parents insisted, and gave him a foundation strong enough to last through the years ahead. He found that in his own home as an adult, the most familiar and comfortable place would be the family altar.

Sam is the oldest of the five boys and two girls born to his parents. He also has an older stepbrother. With that many children, the three bedroom house was always full, but never too crowded for company. His home was a center of hospitality for just about anyone visiting the district.

The agricultural inspector, the schoolteacher, the post-mistress—all were regular faces around the family dinner table. Neighbors and friends were also likely to drop by, giving the house an ongoing atmosphere of fun and fellowship.

Taking part in all those times of laughing, talking, singing, and storytelling, Sam came to believe life is meant to be enjoyed, especially by people who called themselves Christians. He developed a basic belief that life is good. That simple philosophy later grew into a joyful spirit that few circumstances can dampen. He began learning then to base his happiness on God.

As a pastor, he often finds himself saying, "Be jubilant in the Lord, for whatever is in your heart that is good, it is He who has placed it there."

Of all the visitors who came to his home, Sam's favorites were the preachers and seminary students who spent nearly every Sunday afternoon there. Everything about those men interested and inspired him. Wanting to be like them, he studied the things they said and did that set them apart. Even the clerical collar worn by Baptist preachers in Jamaica attracted the impressionable young boy.

Years later friends laughingly call Sam the Baptist Bishop of the Bronx on the occasions when he wears a collar. There are times on his missions field when one must be identified quickly and obviously as a minister. Although it looks unfamiliar to other Southern Baptists, occasionally wearing the collar is more than a statement of identity for Sam. It is also a comfortable reminder of his link to those men in his past.

One young seminary student probably never knew the impact one Sunday afternoon's brief encounter made on Sam. He had gone home with the Simpsons after church for lunch. Before they sat down to eat, he asked Sam's father to gather the family and other guests into the living room. There the student led them in a hymn, read some Scripture verses, and prayed with such feeling it was as if he were talking to another person in the room.

A typical little boy, Sam could not recall all the words the young preacher said in his sermon earlier that morning. But with his call for simple praise and worship that afternoon, he gave Sam a memory that would last a lifetime. He will always strive to provide that kind of spontaneous, warm fellowship in the homes and churches of his adult life.

The more he was exposed to the ministers of his childhood, the more his admiration grew for their sincerity and morality. To that admiration he added a great respect for their positions of authority and leadership.

Long before he was saved, Sam wanted more than anything else in the world to become a preacher. For many years he wondered how he could have had such a deep desire to preach without having had a personal encounter with Jesus Christ. He always thought maybe it was a natural result of his family environment, combined with the role models of past preachers. He came to believe, however, that their influence had been much more prophetic than that.

One day years later he was studying his Bible and reflecting on a verse from the book of Jeremiah.

"Before I formed thee in the belly I knew thee; and before thou camest forth out of the womb I sanctified thee, and ordained thee a prophet unto the nations."

He read the verse again and it spoke directly to his heart. God had known His plans for Sam before he had even come to know God. He had identified so strongly with those preachers, and had such a deep desire to be like them because they shared his purpose in life. He will always believe the preachers he knew as a child had been God's first instruments in revealing that plan to him.

As influential as the preachers and his father had been in his life, his mother played the key role in his salvation experience.

For as long as he could remember, Sam had heard both his mother and father speak of the importance of a personal relationship with Jesus Christ. Slowly, things began to make sense to him, and what he had heard and seen demonstrated in his home began to take on a new meaning.

The realization of his own need to be saved came in a small mission of his home church, as his mother gave the message. Sam found it completely natural to meet her at the front of the church and say that he had decided to give his life to Christ.

As they shared the sweetness of that special moment, the choir was singing in the background, "Where He leads me I will follow, I'll go with him, with him all the way." Neither mother nor son recognized the meaning those words held for their own relationship.

There was nothing Sam could have done to give his mother more joy or pride. She had been praying for this since the day he was born. But his decision and the commitments that were to follow put an ocean between them.

Through the years, visits were never as long or as frequent as either of them wanted. It is a long and expensive trip from New York to Jamaica. But as his ministries grew, it wasn't as much the distance or the money that kept them apart as it was his schedule. The weeks and months slipped by, each one busier than the last. Before he knew it, the time between visits was longer than he had intended.

When one of his churches planned a testimonial dinner for him, someone realized that Sam hadn't seen his mother in five years. They decided the perfect climax of the evening would be a surprise entrance by his mother. All the arrangements were made without his knowledge. When she arrived in New York she was taken to Maisie Bruce's home, well out of his sight. The night of the banquet, she could hardly contain her excitement. The longest part of those five years came during the time she stood in the hallway behind the banquet room, waiting for her cue to enter. Hoping for a glimpse of Sam, she watched through two small square windows in the double doors at the back of the room. People from the church began to filter in and take their seats.

All of a sudden, there he was, laughing and smiling, making his way through the gathering crowd. Tears came to her eyes as she saw that familiar face. Her mind told her that Sam was a grown man now, but her mother's heart was looking at her little boy. Being resigned to life and the fact that children grow up and move away was one thing. But all she could think of right then was reaching her son and feeling her arms around him after five long years.

The minutes crept by until finally the master of ceremonies said the appointed words and she made her entrance. Sam was completely dumbfounded. He knew that something was going on behind the scenes, but never dreamed he would see his mother that night.

It took only an instant for the shock to give way, and he ran from behind the head table to grab his mother and twirl her around. As the audience applauded, he finally received the kisses she had saved for so long.

That evening turned out to be more of a gift to Sam's mother than it was to him. She sat there hearing person after person praise her son for the contributions he was making to the city, the church, and to individual lives. The more she heard, the more she marveled at the completeness of God's plan. Even Sam's earliest endeavors in service had pointed him to his work in New York.

Once his decision for Christ had been made public and he had completed his church's enquirers' class, Sam was baptized. He immediately followed the pattern of involvement set by his parents. He taught Sunday School, joined the choir, and supported the other programs of the church. In all these activities, he took on leadership positions, practicing for his role as pastor.

There was a new awareness about Sam, and as he went to and from church every Sunday, he began to notice a group of children playing in the nearby streets. They weren't that much younger than him, but somehow he felt a sort of fatherly concern for them.

He spoke to his friend Hector, and they decided to begin a Bible class for the children. They began meeting on the steps of a local church with 4 boys and girls. Sam preached and led Bible studies. They met every Sunday afternoon, and in less than six months the group had grown to about 40 children. Technically, he could say that his career in church starting began then.

When he left the group to attend school in Kingston, Barnstaple Anglican Church took over.

His transition to high school meant leaving his rural home behind, and living for the first time in an urban setting. Kingston was a far cry from the small community where he had grown up. He loved the modern, fast-paced feeling of the city. Life was too exciting and his studies too challenging for him to ever realize the permanent break he had made with his rural childhood.

Sam concentrated on two things as he entered high school. First came his studies, and then his ever-present desire to lead those around him. He remained a very actively religious teenager, although that commitment at times wavered in the face of adolescent temptations. An obvious natural leader, he was chosen to be moderator—

a position similar to president—of his class. He also played table tennis, football, and most of all, cricket.

In an effort to be "part of the team," he joined the other boys as they began to experiment with some common teenage rites of passage. Although a few of his friends considered drinking and smoking initiation into adulthood, Sam found that doing those things left him completely unsatisfied with himself, and always unfulfilled.

He soon realized he could hide from his parents, but couldn't escape his own conscience. Neither could he escape his commitment to God. He didn't really want to. In trying to conform, he was losing himself, and he decided that just wasn't worth it.

Sam recommitted himself to Jesus Christ, and has never again deliberately wavered from that decision. He became vice-president of his school's Christian youth movement, and accepted many invitations to other schools and Christian organizations. His desire to preach burned brighter than ever.

After graduating from high school, he spent four years working for the Jamaican Civil Service and traveling around the island. It was a time of great soul-searching and questioning for Sam as he struggled to find the real purpose for his life.

As he earnestly, continually prayed to know the will of God, a familiar answer came. The desire of his heart remained, as it always had been, to become a preacher. But by this point in Sam's life that desire was deeper and more directed. He became more completely aware of God's calling, and the commitment answering that call would involve. With the greatest joy and peace he had ever experienced, Sam said yes to God and began making plans to get the education he would need. Those plans put him on the road that eventually led to the United States.

Like many Jamaicans, Sam has a passion for learning. He loves the challenge of academics. All his life he has found himself returning to the classroom, both as student and as teacher.

After his unsuccessful stint at Emmaus Bible College, he enrolled in Northeastern Bible College, determined to distinguish himself in United States schools as he had in Jamaica.

Obtaining an undergraduate degree from Northeastern was only the beginning. He earned a master's degree from New York Theological Seminary, and then did further studies at two other New York seminaries. An expert on urban ministry and church laity, he became a guest lecturer at Southern Baptist seminaries, as well as a denominational conference leader. He has also spoken in classes at a local Bronx college.

In the process of striving for personal excellence, he was also making his adopted country a better place to live. Although he never sought it, recognition began to come to Sam. In fact, he was so casual about his own accomplishments that in 1974 he almost missed being present for a surprise announcement that he had been named alumnus of the year for Northeastern Bible College.

With Lola's help, the college was able to arrange an entire homecoming ceremony in his honor without his ever knowing. He almost ruined the festivities several times, coming up with a wide range of reasons not to attend homecoming. His parents were here, he had other things to do, there were meetings he would have to cancel. Lola heard and countered every excuse he could think of giving.

"What's the big deal about this homecoming thing?" he asked her time and time again as she kept insisting that they go.

Finally, she convinced him that he needed a nice relaxing day, and that his parents would love to see where he had gone to school.

Sam agreed to go, and even got into the spirit of the occasion. He visited with former teachers, toured the campus, watched the parade, and joined the crowd that gathered to hear the naming of various contest winners.

When the announcement was made that it was time to name the alumnus of the year, he turned to the professor he had been talking with and said, "Who is that, now?"

"Alumnus of the year is Samuel G. Simpson!" he heard over the loudspeaker.

The professor clapped Sam on the back and stepped aside for him to go forward and accept the award. Standing in front of the crowd, he quickly recovered from the shock of the moment and expressed his genuine surprise and gratitude.

But there was plenty of room for him to be humble that day. His mother was there, and she was proud enough for both of them. Nothing her son ever accomplished would surprise her, and there could be no honor too great for him in her eyes. She always had been and always would be his biggest fan.

She was thrilled, but not surprised, in the spring of 1988 when Sam received confirmation that he had been awarded a Merrill Fellowship to the Harvard Divinity School.

He was excited about the possibilities that studying for 13 weeks at Harvard could open in his mind and in his ministries. He had thought long and hard before writing on the fellowship application exactly what issues he was most interested in addressing. Each one posed challenging questions with bearing on the future of his work:

• The role of women in leadership (clerical) position in the church

140

- The mission of the church in a postmodern age
- The relationships between Christian theology and private and public life
- The Christian religion as it relates to other major world religions
- Life-style evangelism and social action

He had decided somewhere back in his childhood to be the best that he could be. That decision has led to a life's philosophy based on striving for excellence. The first three verses of Romans 12 have become a motto for him:

"I beseech you therefore, brethren, by the mercies of God, that ye present your bodies a living sacrifice, holy, acceptable unto God, which is your reasonable service.

"And be not conformed to this world: but be ye transformed by the renewing of your mind, that ye may prove what is that good, and acceptable, and perfect, will of God.

"For I say, through the grace given unto me, to every man that is among you, not to think of himself more highly than he ought to think; but to think soberly, according as God hath dealt to every man the measure of faith."

Sam loves the idea that he does not have to be conformed by the world, to let it squeeze him into its mold. He lives every day in the belief that through the power of the Holy Spirit he can in fact transcend worldliness. His approach to life always goes back to that basic belief that he does not have to live one day in defeat, but really can live in victory.

The little Jamaican farm boy has come a long way since his days of observing the local preachers and wanting to be like them. His ministry is as different from theirs as New York City is from Jamaica. Sam found his own personal calling, and is accomplishing his own unique purposes. But God has used the things Sam learned from those early days to help build His work in the Bronx.

Sam Simpson has adopted America. But Jamaica will always be the home of roots that were strong enough to take him where God wanted him to go. When he left his island home in 1959, he had every intention of returning there, once he was trained and ready to make his contribution. Then, when he left Chicago questioning his entire future, one of the things that bothered him the most was the prospect of returning home a failure. Sam's fear was never realized, and he has gone home many times as the preacher he left to become. But in 1980 something unexpected happened that gave him one of his greatest experiences of personal satisfaction. That year he was named one of only four recipients from Canada and the United States to receive the Air Jamaica Award of Excellence.

The government-owned airline gives the award in recognition of outstanding accomplishments native Jamaicans make to their new countries. The focus of the award is not on what the recipients achieve for themselves, but what they do in serving others.

Sam found that a familiar island saying best described his reaction to being chosen to receive such an award.

"It makes you feel good all over," he would say, smiling.

But this time he was doing more than offering his usual quip. That one little saying did express much of the way he felt. Being brought back home and acknowledged for the life's work he had chosen in his new country had a satisfying completeness.

The meaning behind this award spoke to his heart. Through it he felt his homeland saying, "You are making your contribution to Jamaica. You're just doing it there instead of here." Sam was deeply touched.

He and Lola were flown to Jamaica for several days of activities, culminating in the awards presentation. The ceremony took place in one of the island's most exclusive hotels. Chamber music played as they ate an elaborate eight-course dinner. Then the lights dimmed and the meal's dramatic finale came with the entrance of a giant cake encircled by blue flames. It was quite an evening.

The Jamaican ambassador came from Washington, as did the United Nations representative from New York. The guest speaker was the island's governor general, and the wife of the prime minister made the presentation.

Sitting in the audience as his guests were Sam's mother, other members of his family, and some of his fellow Jamaican ministers. These were the people who had seen him come full circle. They appreciated more than anyone what that night meant to him.

When his turn came to speak, Sam chose his words carefully.

Receiving this award, he said, was not an accomplishment, but a blessing.

"I must forever be mindful that God has enabled everything that I have achieved . . . and to be quickly reminded that pride comes from success and achievement."

He knows that power comes with acknowledgement and acceptance, and constantly reminds himself that anything good that happens is from God.

"Power without God, recognition without God is extreme poverty in any life," he said.

Sam didn't know how long he had been leaning against that car, lost in thoughts of Jamaica and what the years had brought. All of a sudden he remembered what had started him on his trip back to Jamaica, and he noticed that the children who had been playing in the water were gone. They had turned off the hydrant and moved on to some other game. The cement surrounding it was wet, and darker than the rest of the sidewalk. But in the heat of New York City's afternoon sun, that dark spot was slowly fading away. Before long, there wouldn't be any evidence left of what those children had been doing.

Sam smiled to himself. He knew that they would remember their game and come back again another day.

Chapter 10

The heat of the afternoon had given way to a warm night breeze. Sam stood on the sidewalk in front of Bronx Baptist Church, greeting people as they began to arrive for the Sunday evening service. It was a perfect night for their open-air street meeting.

He looked around the corner and saw Amy, the young summer missionary from Oklahoma, driving the Wake-Eden van toward the church. The windows were open, and as the van passed, he could hear what sounded like all the missionaries talking at once. It was a quick burst of voices, almost like opening a door to a party and closing it right behind you.

After Amy parked the van behind the church, the missionaries came walking down the sidewalk toward him. They were talking and laughing with their usual enthusiasm. Tonight was their last Sunday in the Bronx. Ten weeks had come and gone, and now they were seasoned, homesick summer missionaries. Most of them had already packed their suitcases, and were ready to leave.

Sam would be sorry to see them go. He had not spent as much time with them as he would have liked. But his churches had felt the effects of their service.

Besides the help they provided every day with the children, just having them there had been encouraging to the regular workers. Their spirit of eager cooperation and genuine desire to minister had been a good influence. This group had succeeded in their efforts to fit into the existing life-style and needs structure of the Bronx.

He hated to see their work end for these reasons and more. What he would really miss, he had told them at a farewell cookout on Friday night, would be having eight willing partners in crime on his Sunday night excursions to the local ice-cream stand.

"Amy, my good friend, how are you doing this fine evening?" Sam asked as she walked toward him.

"I'm fine, Pastor," Amy said, not in her usual bubbly tone.

"And how was our beautiful lady in the harbor?" he asked. The missionaries spent their last Saturday in New York sightseeing. They had saved going to the Statue of Liberty as a finale to their trip. He had heard Amy talk off and on all summer about going there. The statue had been the symbol of New York City to her, and she couldn't wait to see it.

"Oh, it was pretty cool," she said, but Sam could tell something more was on her mind.

When they first arrived in the Bronx Sam told the missionaries to feel free to come to him with any problems they might be having. But he had been so busy they seldom approached him with more than a quick question. Now it seemed obvious Amy wanted to talk to him about something, but wasn't quite sure how to bring it up.

"Would you mind helping me get some hymnbooks out of my office for us to use tonight?" he asked, giving Amy a chance to talk to him in private if she wanted.

As they went inside and he rummaged around in some cabinets for the hymnals, Sam asked a few more questions

146

that would give her an opening to share what was on her mind.

"Pastor, something happened," she said, starting to move a stack of papers out of a chair so that she could sit down. In the middle of her sentence she stopped, and put the papers back where they had been. "Oh, I don't know what I'm thinking of. You probably need to be going over your sermon or something right now."

"No, no, it's not my turn to preach tonight," he said, sitting down behind the desk as if he had all the time in the world.

Sunday evening services were almost completely conducted by the laypeople of his churches. He preached occasionally, but usually a member of the congregation, or some visiting Southern Baptist pastor or volunteer would deliver the evening message. A couple of the summer missionaries had even taken a turn.

"Now, what happened?"

"Well, it was nothing bad. It's just something that I can't get out of my mind," Amy said.

The missionaries had spent the whole day sightseeing, going all over New York. Everyone had a great time, and they ended the night by splurging on an expensive dinner at a fancy restaurant. It was the kind of day they had been looking forward to all summer as they coped with heat and children and fatigue.

Everyone had been in high spirits when they boarded the subway for the long ride back to the Bronx. It was late and there were few people in their subway car, so they all had plenty of room to sit together.

But Amy went down to the other end of the car, where a distinguished looking elderly black man sat by himself. It wasn't unusual for the missionaries to use opportunities such as a subway ride to talk with the people around them. She hadn't really planned on witnessing that night, but something about the man made her want to talk to him. Even after ten weeks in New York, she had never seen such a blank, cold look on anyone's face.

She could tell by the man's clothes that he was poor, yet there was a certain air of dignity about him. He sat completely erect, wearing round, scholarly glasses and a Dobson straw hat. His frayed shirt and thin cotton pants showed the recent crease of an iron. Amy estimated that he was about 80 years old.

After a couple of attempts to start a conversation, she managed to get him to tell her his name.

"Moses," was his curt, but not hostile, reply.

As the subway train rocked and the rest of the missionaries sat laughing together at the other end of the car, she began telling him about Jesus. Some of his coldness melted, but not to receive her message. His blank look disappeared only to reveal the pain that blocked her words.

He began to argue with what she was saying, finally slamming his fist on his knee and demanding to know how there could even be a God, when he and other black people had suffered so.

Amy was a middle-class white college student from Oklahoma. She had no idea what kind of suffering he had experienced during the past 80 years. She had never felt the feelings or known the despair that he was describing. There was no common ground between the two of them, other than Jesus. But their differences didn't even enter her mind. All she could see was a person who desperately needed love and hope.

Ever since the day she had been with the group Pastor Simpson had taken on a tour of the Bronx, Amy had been redefining her purpose in being there. Soon after that tour she had been working in the church one afternoon when the pastor came in with a group of men and a couple of women. They were Southern Baptist volunteers who had just arrived for a week of sweat evangelism. As he talked to them about their mission, his words caught Amy's attention. She stopped cutting out construction paper apples and strained to hear more from her nearby workroom.

"And one day we will say of a burned-out Bronx, 'Yesterday's impossibility has become today's possibility,' because a group of Christians known as Southern Baptists came north, gave up their racist attitude toward people, and in boldness under God, erected a bridge upon which people walked by the aid of the Holy Spirit to help others in distress.

"The only permanent bridge to a burned-out Bronx is Jesus Christ. We are walking together, Christian brothers and sisters, on that bridge!"

Listening to him, Amy had been able to visualize her world, connected to the Bronx by Jesus. After that day, every time she talked to someone or ministered to them in any way, she could see herself walking across that bridge to meet them.

And she felt the bridge of Christ's love firmly providing her only support as she patiently tried to answer the questions of that bitter old man. She finally told him that she didn't have all the answers, but she did know that Jesus died for him, and loved him.

He just looked away. But when the train stopped at 180th Street and he got up to leave, the man turned back to Amy for just an instant. He didn't say anything, but she could see tears streaming down his cheeks. Then the doors closed behind him, and the train moved on. She knew she would never see him again.

Amy had sat there thinking about how a person could be so hurt by man that he couldn't believe in anybody or anything. She was convinced God could still reach him, even through the hardness of his heart. As she thanked

God for using her to plant the seed, she prayed that although she would never see it, one day He would give the increase and Mr. Moses would be saved.

"So I guess what I wanted to tell you, Pastor, was that it just kind of shook me up to realize I'd never be able to see New York, or, well, a lot of things, the same way again," Amy told Sam as she finished her story.

After spending a summer living with the reality of city missions, all her illusions were gone. She had dealt with the city—the poor, the homeless, the ethnic, the indifferent, the hopeless. But she could no longer fit faceless groups into her missions field. Where she had seen the challenge of issues before, all she could see now was the need of individuals.

And for the rest of her life, when she thought of New York City, it would be in terms of an 80-year-old black man named Moses.

She and Sam stopped right then to pray for him, wherever he was out in the night.

"You know, Amy, you've learned a powerful lesson, one that it took me quite a while, as a missionary and a pastor, to learn," he said.

It was true they would never know what became of Moses, and what effect her words had had on him.

"But God doesn't call us to win everybody we meet. What He does call us to do, however, is minister to them," he said.

He has experienced that truth in his own ministry. While his ultimate goal is in seeing souls saved, he gives his daily attention to reaching that goal through healing broken bodies and broken spirits.

Watching the Bronx deteriorate past what looked like the point of no return had helped him understand his mission, and the mission of his churches. As the government and the rest of the country neglect the needs of people caught in the disaster, he has seen social and moral problems skyrocket.

In failing to care about the burning buildings of the Bronx, the world fails to care about the people who occupied those buildings. Burned-out buildings began to be echoed by burned-out human spirits. As people lost their sense of dignity and self-worth, they began turning to other things—whatever it took —to make them feel good.

Crime and drugs all too often provide the most readily available escape from their world of frustration and poverty. No one living in that world is safe, or free. Even some children carry knives and guns to school.

And in the midst of it all, Sam stands with his churches, offering another, more permanent way for the people of the Bronx to feel good about themselves. He leads his churches to show these people a Jesus Who is more than just a name to take in vain or a symbol of some religious past. Through the ministries of Sam Simpson's churches, Jesus Christ has become a living door to new life for many of those people.

He doesn't see any limit to what God can do, as long as they remain faithful.

"What is the priority of your life?" he often asks his congregations.

"The priority of my life is to let the glow from heaven come down and flush itself through me. Because Heaven is in me, and I live on earth, where I walk the light of Jesus Christ shines!"

Sam dreams of the day that light will shine into all parts of the Bronx, and radiate out from there to the rest of New York City. He is a practical man living in a realistic world. But still he believes that the power of God can reach even the darkest places the world has devised to hide human hearts from His love.

The people on his missions field who are most in need

of the gospel aren't likely to come to a church service looking for it. But they might come in search of a free meal, or help in finding a decent place to live, or a good school for their children. If he can get them that far, the demonstration of a living gospel will do the rest, he is convinced.

And if they can't or won't even come that far, he believes in going to them. He'll extend his ministries into the community, into the prisons, into the youth gangs, into the apartment buildings—wherever he can find a foothold. He'll even take his churches out into the streets, literally, if that is what it takes to share the hope of Jesus Christ.

Sam often refers to Nehemiah when challenging his churches to reach out into their city. He leads the people to draw many conclusions from the story of that prophet and his concern for another city.

"When the Jewish people returned from captivity in Babylon, they found the city of Jerusalem in ruins. The walls were still broken down and the gates had not been restored since the time they were burned.

"When Nehemiah learned about the condition of his city and his people, he sat down and wept.

"His sitting down and weeping showed that human hopelessness and helplessness confronted him. He did what came naturally. He wept.

"The lesson we might learn here is that you never lighten the load unless first you have felt the pressure in your own soul. He wept over the ruined city. At another time, Jesus himself wept over Jerusalem.

"Secondly, he refused to eat for several days. His humanity came through, his concern, his compassion.

"Thirdly, he spent time talking to God. What is so important about Nehemiah's conversation with God is that having prayed, he in turn listened to God.

"He obeyed God, and no one could move him from doing that which God had instructed him to do. And God opened the door on his behalf. As a matter of fact, God went ahead and opened doors of opportunity for him.

"My friends, we are all a part of the human family, and when one suffers, we all suffer. When there is a family who is homeless, who is hungry and even hopeless on the streets of New York, we all suffer. And when our earthly resources are insufficient to meet the human need, we have to turn to resources from the God of Heaven, Who will go ahead and make the way clear.

"Nehemiah was called, prepared, and placed by God for the rebuilding of the walls of Jerusalem. Can our call be any less for the rebuilding of bodies and spirits in the city of New York?"

Through the years God has proven to Sam that when He gives a vision, He will also give someone to help make that vision a reality. Since the first days of his ministry, Sam has been challenging people to share his dream of a better world.

He challenged a handful of people at Honeywell Avenue to see a vision instead of a slum. They did, and now he challenges two churches and three missions to a future that will far surpass the victories of their past. Why not have Bible studies and then churches in every one of the Bronx's 16 community districts? Why not target language or cult groups and start 15, 20, 25, or more Bible studies among them? Why not buy three and one-half acres of land for $6 million and build a church, a school, and a community center?

Why not, he says, do what it takes to win a place like the Bronx, New York, for the kingdom of God?

Sam believes that nowhere is the richness of God's creation more beautifully displayed than in the diversity of New York City. The complexity and variety of life offered there is a reflection of His handiwork. He realizes that spectrum of beauty is mirrored by an equal display of ugliness and sin. What he wants to magnify, through God, is the beauty.

To do that, he joins hands with anyone who will share his vision. He points to the words of Jesus as He prayed for unity among the Christians who would carry out His work:

"That they all may be one, as thou Father art in me, and I in Thee, that they also may be one in us, that the world may believe that thou hast sent me."

He calls his own church members to discover and use their individual gifts in ministering to those around them. They don't have to be like someone else, their church doesn't have to be like any other. All they have to do is be faithful to who and what God has called them to be.

Because Sam has given them the freedom to use those gifts in obedience to God, their ministries have blossomed and multiplied. And time after time those ministering have reaped more benefit than those who received their ministry.

This has been the case for thousands of Southern Baptists, as they put away preconceived ideas and prejudices, differences in opinion and doctrine, to join the fight to save the Bronx. What they find is often so different from what they expected that Sam is never quite sure at first if they are more frightened or relieved.

The groups of volunteers, especially those who have never been to New York City before, often remind him of Stephen's reaction when Lola went to Africa.

When he was a young boy, she had gone to a conference in Africa with a group from the United Nations. Sam was going to join her after the conference, and they were to tour several countries. One morning several days after Lola left, she called to check on things at home. It was so early that he didn't wake the children to talk to her.

Later, when they got up, Sam told them that their mother had called that morning from Africa.

"Oh, you mean our mother is alive?" Stephen asked.

"Well, of course! What in the world do you mean, Stephen?" his father asked.

"I just figured a lion would have eaten her by now," he said.

He was greatly relieved that his mother was alive, and that a lion had not eaten her. But he could hardly believe that he was wrong about the Africa he had imagined all his life—a dangerous, mysterious place full of dark jungles and ferocious lions. On one hand the truth was comforting, but on the other he hated to give up his exotic Africa.

Sam made sure that he and Lola took lots of pictures showing the many sides of African life, from women carrying water pots on their heads to highways filled with cars, from mud huts to exclusive vacation resorts.

Just as there is no simple picture of African life, Sam knows there isn't one simple view of life in New York City. And as Stephen had been both relieved and perplexed to find his imagination in conflict with reality, so are many of the volunteers.

But like Stephen, all of them come away from the experience much wiser and more mature in their understanding. Once they get used to the idea, they are glad to let go of the city and the mission they had imagined. They find dealing with the complexities of reality much more satisfying. That satisfaction is what keeps bringing more teams of volunteers to the Bronx year after year.

Sam and Amy were still talking when someone came to the open door and said there was a man from Georgia who needed to see the pastor.

As Amy started to go, she turned back to Sam and said, "If I don't get another chance to tell you, thanks for everything. A lot of times I thought it was terrible, but now I know, I mean, well, it's just been worth everything.'' She stopped, at a loss for the words to express her feelings.

''Amy, just take what you've learned and help somebody else see the purpose God might have in places or circumstances they don't understand,'' he said.

They could hear the sound of a piano playing outside before they opened the church's basement door. It was twilight, and a few of the church members were beginning to sit down in the metal chairs Sam had helped put out that afternoon. He was surprised to see Lola on the second row, and he waved to her.

The Sons of Jubilee, ministers of music from Georgia, stood on the platform in front of the chairs, practicing. Their leader saw Sam, and motioned for him to come and answer a few of their questions about the order of service. He found the man who was in charge of the program and they went over to the platform.

Sam reminded them to ''sing loud,'' saying they never knew who might be listening. He told them about the night they had had a singing group at one of Wake-Eden's open-air meetings. He had been delayed, and was still at home when the group began singing.

They were several blocks away, but he could hear them inside his house. He was surprised the sound carried that far. But he was even more surprised to hear, on the other side of the duplex, his neighbor singing along with the Baptist hymns.

It was almost time for tonight's service to start, so Sam slipped into the seat next to Lola. He would introduce the program, but after that the laymen conducted everything.

''What are you doing here? I thought you had to study,'' he asked.

The last time he had seen Lola, she was standing in front of the kitchen sink, washing dishes and saying,

"Praise the Lord, oh my soul, and all that is within me."

Whenever his wife felt under pressure or distressed, he would hear her saying those words over and over to herself. And usually, she would be standing at the sink.

Washing dishes was where Lola did her heaviest thinking. With her hands busy and her mind free, it was often there that she received her greatest insights.

She had been praising God in order to remove the pressures of her life for so long that she wasn't even aware anymore when she was doing it. But it was a dead giveaway to Sam that something bothered her. Tonight the problem was a lack of sleep and two nursing finals facing her tomorrow. A serious student, she worried about being prepared.

Just before Sam left she told him she thought she'd better stay home and study. That was why he was surprised to see her.

"I just decided I wanted to be here tonight," she told Sam as the service started.

He understood what she meant. There was something about these street meetings that made them unlike any other ministry of their churches. Here they took the gospel outside the walls of the church, and literally threw the message to the wind.

Standing to announce the night's program, Sam noticed there was a relatively small crowd seated in the metal chairs. But he smiled to himself, remembering last week when he had preached for the Honeywell mission. Their open-air service was held in the street outside the Shepherd's 340 Building, one of the poorest neighborhoods in the Bronx.

That night the small congregation from the mission had been dwarfed by the huge apartment buildings hovering around them. Only one or two people from the community joined the group for the evening service.

But as the youth choir started singing, Sam had looked around and seen quite a crowd.

On the street, men stood smoking cigarettes and leaning against their cars. Mothers seeking a cool breeze sat on the steps outside apartment buildings, rocking their babies in time to the music. High above them, many people leaned out their windows, listening. Even inside some apartments, people turned off radios and televisions so they could hear what was going on outside.

This was strictly "come as you are" church. Most of the listeners wore shorts and T-shirts, some even pajamas. They were cooking dinner or folding clothes or reading the newspaper. Some were drinking beer, or worse. But whatever they were doing, it was hard not to hear the words *Jesus* and *love* and *hope*.

In the street below, people were singing at the top of their lungs. The quality of their music may have suffered slightly because of the volume, but they had to be loud to be heard. The testimonies were shouted, as was the sermon. Their noisy witness gave the message a boost as it took to the air.

And with that little extra boost, a beautiful thing happened. The words would just float along, anywhere the air wanted to take them. The gospel fell on listening ears as it drifted into the surrounding cars and apartments.

People passing by would not have seen the gathered crowd. But Sam did, and as far as he was concerned they were just as much visitors in the church as if they had walked through the doors. The street became the pulpit, and the pews had been replaced with cars and stoops and open windows.

Like many of the ministries reaching out to the people of the city, there was more to this service than met the eye. The casual observer couldn't look at the surface and see what was really happening.

Even Sam, as he stood preaching to the darkened cars, brick walls, and open windows, was not aware of the dramatic changes going on in at least two of the apartments overhead.

In one a woman leaned out the window as far as she dared, straining to hear the words being spoken. She had never been to the chapel on Honeywell Avenue, but she had been aware of the street meetings beneath her window for several weeks. Sometimes she listened, sometimes she didn't. But tonight she couldn't keep herself from listening, and something strange took place inside her heart. Things she had heard before but never understood began to make sense, in a strange and exciting way.

In another apartment on the same side of the building, another woman sat at her kitchen table, right next to the open window. She had had her head in her hands, but now she was covering her ears as she tried not to hear the words coming up from the street. They felt as if they were boring into her soul. She wanted to get up, close the window, go into another room. But she couldn't. The more she heard, the more convicted she became. Even her crying wasn't loud enough to drown out those words.

Finally, the preaching stopped. Patiently, clearly, Sam capsulized his message, inviting the hearers one last time to come forward and give their lives to Christ.

The invitation hymn started, and a few Christians came forward to kneel on the sidewalk. As the Christians prayed for the lost people all around them who had heard the message, one had already asked Jesus to come into her heart. Another still sat struggling at her kitchen table. As they prayed for decisions, two women were making theirs.

Sam stood in the middle of the street in one of the poorest neighborhoods in one of the most godless cities in the world. He could not see inside the hearts of the people around him anymore than he could see inside the brick walls that hid them.

He could not know that inside one of those buildings, two women were making their way toward salvation right now. He could not know that two more souls were about to be added to the kingdom of Heaven. He could not know that at that moment angels were preparing to build two more mansions on the street he had started.

All he knew for sure as he looked into the blackness of a New York City night was that he was where God had placed him, and nowhere in the world was more exciting.

Just then Sam saw two women crossing the street and coming in his direction. Smiling, he held out a hand to each of them.

Sam Simpson networks with many people in his job as a Southern Baptist home missionary.

Worshipers gather at Bronx Baptist Church.

Bronx Baptist Church is one of the two churches Sam pastors in New York City.

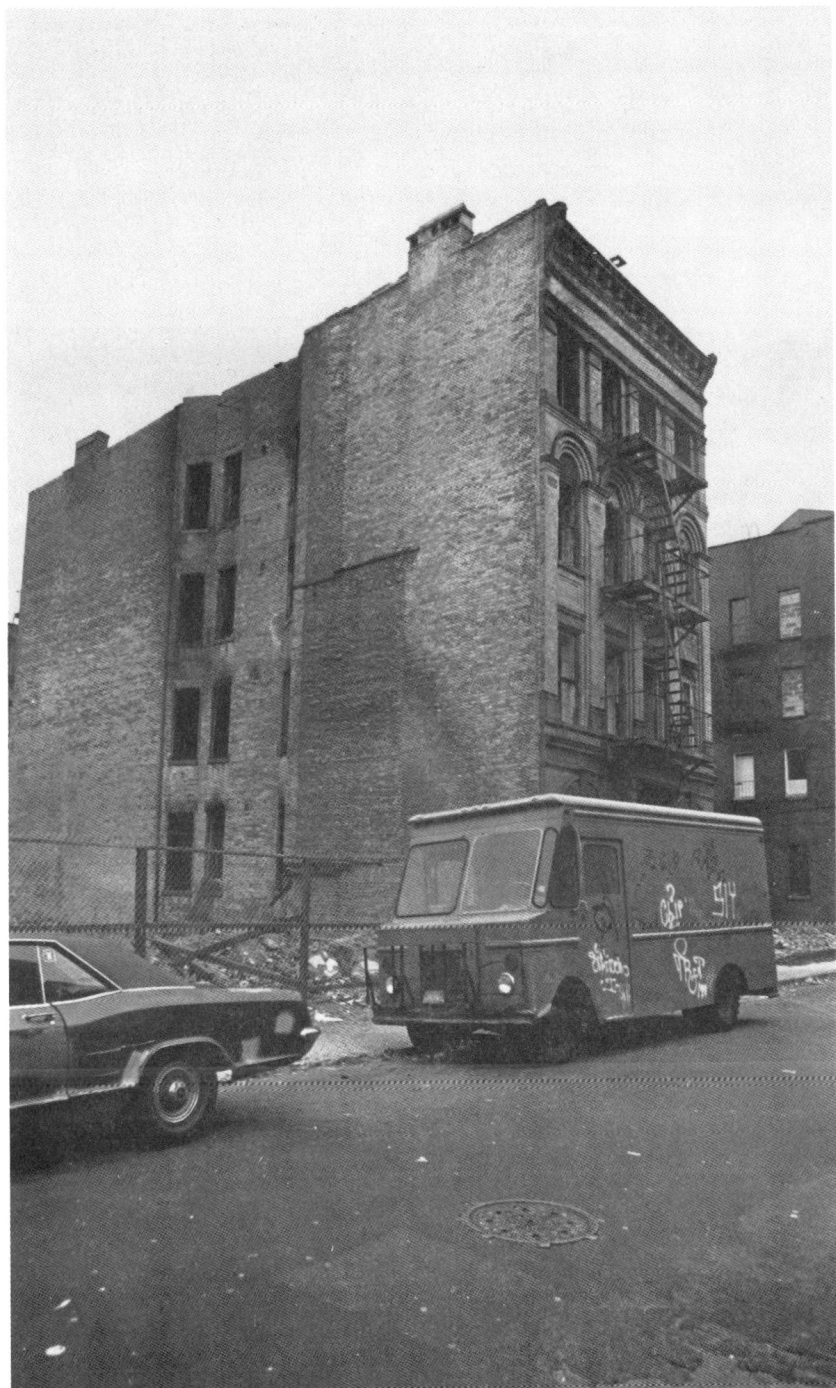

Renovating buildings is a vital part of Sam's ministry. People in the Bronx are provided with decent homes as well as the gospel.

Sam and Lola Simpson meet Rev. and Mrs. Desmond Tutu and Rev. William McCulmont. During his years in the Bronx, Sam has built relationships that span the globe.

Sam and Lola on their wedding day in 1963.

Sam and Lola with their children, Kim, Erica, and Stephen, in a recent photograph.

Sam and Dan Nickerson of the Shepherds Corporation inspect a building site.

Wake-Eden Community Baptist Church, also pastored by Sam, is located in a middle-class section of the Bronx.

STUDY GUIDE

Joyce S. Martin

Part 1—Group Study

Before the Study

1. Publicize the study. Use announcements, church bulletins and newsletters, and bulletin boards to advertise the study. Use maps of New York City with the Bronx highlighted and posters with the book title *Sam Simpson: Architect of Hope,* date, time, and place of the study on them. Check libraries and atlases for maps.

2. Read *Sam Simpson: Architect of Hope* in its entirety. Prepare a minilecture to introduce Sam and Lola Simpson and the Bronx using chapters 1 and 7. Prepare to tell two or three favorite stories not included in the teaching plan below (or enlist participants to tell the stories).

3. Establish your learning objectives. At the completion of this study, each person will have

   a) Become acquainted with the ministry of Sam Simpson.

   b) Developed an appreciation for home missionaries like Sam Simpson who minister in difficult places.

   c) Compared and contrasted stereotypes about the Bronx and those who live and minister there with the actual facts.

   d) Prepared a list of specific things for which they will pray concerning Sam Simpson and the people in the Bronx.

4. Collect resources needed for the study. These include copies of *Sam Simpson: Architect of Hope,* a map of New York City, a world map with a ribbon marker from Jamaica to Chicago to New York City, paper, pencils, felt-tip markers, sentence strips, a recording of "Because He Lives" (*Baptist Hymnal,* 1975 edition) (or enlist someone to play the song on the piano), and a recording of Jamaican music.

5. Enlist persons who will coordinate snack time during the intermission. Use the recipes below, or check your local library or bookstore for other recipes.

JAMAICAN FRUIT BOWL

Select a wide assortment of fresh fruits. Cut into chunks. Pour one can of sweetened condensed milk over the fruit just prior to serving.

JAMAICAN RICE AND BEANS

3 cups rice
1 cup red peas (beans)
a pinch of thyme
1 fresh coconut
a pinch of salt

¼ teaspoon black pepper
1 clove garlic
2 stalks scallions,
   grated or one small
   onion, grated
2 quarts water

Grate coconut. Use water to express milk from coconut by adding 2 cups water at a time and squeezing milk through a sieve after each addition until water is finished.

Place peas (beans) in saucepan with coconut milk. Add garlic, slightly crushed. Cook until peas are tender but not overcooked. Add salt, thyme, rice, and 2 cups water with each 1 cup rice. Cook over medium heat, covered, stirring twice, until rice is cooked.

JAMAICAN PEPPERPOT

1 pound kale, ground
1 pound cabbage, ground
1½ pounds beef, cubed and
   cooked
½ pound cooked chicken
½ pound cooked corned
   beef
1 cup coconut
12 okra, cut

2 onions, ground
1 quart chicken stock
½ teaspoon salt
½ teaspoon thyme
½ teaspoon cayenne
2 green onions, sliced
1 pod garlic
2 tablespoons
   Worcestershire sauce

Combine all ingredients except okra. Cook over low heat for 1½ hours. Add okra and continue cooking until tender.

6. Construct a backdrop representing the Bronx. To make the backdrop, cut two strips from rolls of butcher paper or paper tablecloth. Tape them together vertically. Then sketch in a scene to represent the Bronx—include both the South Bronx and the affluent areas of the Bronx. Use pictures from *Sam Simpson: Architect of Hope* to draw dilapidated high-rise apartment buildings, the Bronx Baptist Church, Wake-Eden Community Baptist Church, and other structures. Display the backdrop on the meeting room wall. Display the maps of New York City and of the world.

7. Prepare a poster that says *Sam Simpson: Architect of Hope*.

8. Enlist persons to represent Maisie Bruce, Ray and Frances

168

Boggs, Hyacynthe, and a member of the Shepherds Restoration Corporation whom you (or someone whom you will designate prior to the session) will interview during the study session. Give a copy of the interview guide below to each interviewee before the session. Each interviewee will also need a copy of *Sam Simpson: Architect of Hope* with appropriate pages marked: Bruce—chapter 2; Boggs—pages 72-75; Hyacynthe—pages 42-46; Shepherds—chapters 4 and 5.

INTERVIEW GUIDE
a) How long have you worked with Rev. Simpson?
b) How did you first become involved in ministry in the Bronx?
c) Tell us about your ministry in the Bronx.
d) What are the joys you have experienced in your work?
e) What are some of the heartaches you have experienced?
f) How has your Bronx ministry changed your life?

9. Prepare the following materials for use during the study.
    a) Work sheet for each participant

Sam Simpson: Architect of Hope
Complete the work sheet using the listed pages from the book as reference to discover how Sam's personal characteristics help him overcome specific obstacles to ministry.

Sam's Traits	Specific Obstacles	How These Help Sam Overcome Obstacles
Healthy ego, confident (p. 7)		
Blended preaching style (p. 12)		
Makes friends easily (p. 14)		
Strong faith in God (p. 15)		
Takes time to laugh (p. 21)		

169

Delegates (p. 27)

Open to every possibility to meet needs of others (p. 32)

Optimistic, but realistic (p. 35, 115)

Uses resources he has (p. 41)

Advocate for poor (p. 42, 47-48)

Risk taker (p. 60)

Learns through difficulties (p. 97)

  b) Quote placards
   Write each of the following quotes on separate sentence strips.

1. "A very strong personality, it is his nature to be confident."
2. "And most of all, he never forgets that he is just a man, struggling with life like everybody else."
3. "Such a God," Sam thought, "to put me in a place like the Bronx and make it home in my heart."
4. "To Sam Simpson, rebuilding a life means renewing human dignity as well as rescuing a soul."
5. "They (the Shepherds) knew that their churches, perhaps better than anyone, understood the kinds of needs most urgent out in the community."

  c) Prayer cards entitled "Today I Will Pray for the Bronx." Participants will write prayer concerns on these cards.

 10. Enlist three persons to read one Scripture verse each: Jeremiah 29:7, Isaiah 35:1, and Jeremiah 29:11. Write each verse on a separate sentence strip.
 11. Enlist someone to present a monologue based on Amy, the summer missionary mentioned in chapters 2, 5, and 10.

At the Study

1. As participants arrive, play a recording of "Because He Lives." Lead them in singing the chorus of this song.

2. Welcome: Use this introduction:

Welcome to the Bronx, one of the five boroughs of New York City. The Bronx, taking her place proudly alongside Manhattan, Queens, Brooklyn, and Staten Island to form New York City, our nation's largest metropolitan area. The Bronx, chiefly a residential area extending along the Hudson River north of Manhattan. The Bronx, 42 square miles—more people than the states of North Dakota and Vermont combined. The Bronx, over 27,000 persons crowded into each square mile.

3. Brainstorm (10 minutes): Point out the backdrop representing the Bronx. Lead participants in brainstorming their first reactions when they hear the word *Bronx*. Write their responses on sentence strips and tape to the backdrop.

Tape the poster that says *Sam Simpson: Architect of Hope* to the backdrop. Ask: What characteristics do you think a missionary needs in order to effectively minister in the Bronx? List those on sentence strips and tape to the left side of the poster.

4. Minilecture—Meet Sam Simpson (20 minutes): Introduce Sam Simpson and his ministry in the Bronx by using material in chapters 1 and 7. Focus on how Sam came to the United States from Jamaica and specifically how he came to the Bronx. Tell how he met his wife, Lola.

Describe both the South Bronx in which the Bronx Baptist Church is located and Wake-Eden the section of the Bronx in which the Wake-Eden Community Baptist Church is located. Describe the burned-out sections of Charlotte Street in the South Bronx and the fashionable Riverdale and Co-Op City areas. Talk about how one's first response to the word *Bronx* includes only the South Bronx. Contrast these areas with Sam's homeland of Jamaica.

Tell participants that during this study they will learn more about Sam and about the Bronx through meeting persons with whom Sam works. Tell them to listen for barriers to ministry in the Bronx and for characteristics which Sam and those who work with him possess which help them minister effectively in the Bronx in spite of those obstacles.

5. Interview (20 minutes): Introduce pre-enlisted persons who will represent Maisie Bruce, Ray and Frances Boggs, Hyacynthe, and a member of the Shepherds. Interview them using prepared questions.

6. Intermission (15 minutes): Serve Jamaican snacks and play recordings of Jamaican music, if available.

7. Music: Play the recording "Because He Lives" to cue participants that it's time for the study to begin.

8. Study Groups (35 minutes): Form study groups of five members each. Provide copies of the book. Give each group member a copy of the work sheet entitled *Sam Simpson: Architect of Hope.* Instruct each group to elect a leader and a recorder/reporter. Allow 30 minutes for the groups to complete their research.

Call on reporters to share what obstacles Sam has faced to ministry in the Bronx. Lead the group to compare their first brainstorming impressions of the Bronx to this list of actual conditions in the Bronx. Lead group members to choose five of the obstacles which they think are the most difficult. Write these on sentence strips and add to backdrop next to members' brainstorming list.

Ask reporters to share what group members have learned about why Sam has been able to overcome the obstacles to ministry. Lead the group to compare their first brainstorming list of characteristics needed to minister in the Bronx to this list of Sam's traits. Lead group members to choose five of Sam's characteristics which they think are key to his successful ministry in the Bronx. Write these on sentence strips and add to right side of poster entitled *Sam Simpson: Architect of Hope.*

9. Story Time (20 minutes): Tell in story fashion two or three (as time permits) of your favorite stories from the book (alternate: pre-enlist participants to tell these stories).

10. Quotes (10 minutes): Display the quote sentence strips on the wall. Ask volunteers to each read a quote. Lead a discussion of how these quotes show characteristics all missionaries need.

11. Seeing the Bronx Through God's Eyes (10 minutes): Ask pre-enlisted persons to read Jeremiah 29:7, Isaiah 35:1, and Jeremiah 29:11, in that order. Place the sentence strips with those verses written on them over the backdrop of the Bronx. Summarize the study by leading a discussion of how Sam and those with whom he works have been able to see hope blossoming in the wasteland of the South Bronx.

Introduce the person who will give the monologue of Amy, the missionary, who came to see the Bronx through God's eyes after spending a summer there.

12. The Bronx—Now What Do You See? (10 minutes): Briefly summarize chapter 10. Re-read the list of first reactions to the word *Bronx.* Ask participants how they have modified their thinking about the Bronx during the study. Talk about how stereotypes and misinformation can threaten or destroy ministry. Talk about how participants can pray more effectively for Sam and his ministry now that they know the facts. Talk about how all missionaries need the characteristics Sam ex-

emplifies. Encourage participants to read the book.

Give each participant a prayer card. Ask them to list prayer needs for the Bronx and for the Simpsons for which they will pray. To conclude the study session, ask participants to pray sentence prayers for these needs.

Part 2—Individual Study

1. Make a list of your first impressions when you hear the word *Bronx.*

2. Make a list of the characteristics you think a missionary would need in order to minister effectively in the Bronx.

3. Read the book *Sam Simpson: Architect of Hope* and the learning objectives in the group study plan (p. 167).

4. After reading the book, make a second list of facts concerning the Bronx. Compare this list with the list you made in question 1.

5. Make a list of characteristics of Sam Simpson which you think have helped make him effective in his ministry in the Bronx. Compare this list with the list you made in question 2.

6. Complete the work sheet entitled *Sam Simpson: Architect of Hope* in the group study guide.

7. Complete the activity "Quotes" from the group study guide.

8. Read Jeremiah 29:7, Isaiah 35:1, and Jeremiah 29:11. Re-read chapter 10 of the book. Write an essay summarizing how Sam Simpson and the people of the Bronx Baptist and Wake-Eden Baptist churches have seen hope blossoming in the wasteland of the South Bronx.

9. Write a summary of one of your favorite stories from the book.

10. Tell the story you chose in question 9 to a friend.

11. Re-read your list of first reactions to the word *Bronx.* Write your answers to the following questions:

   a) How does this list reflect stereotypes?

   b) How has your view of the Bronx remained the same or changed as a result of reading this book?

12. Write your answer to the following questions:

   a) What principles for dealing with stereotypes have you learned from reading this book?

   b) What principles for overcoming obstacles to ministry have you learned from reading this book?

   c) What situations in your own community need to be addressed by someone like Sam Simpson?

   d) How are you in your own community an "architect of hope"?

e) How can you in your own community be a more effective architect of hope? In what situations do you specifically need to get involved?

13. Write a prayer list of needs in the Bronx and in the ministry of Sam Simpson. Based on your study of the ministry of Rev. Simpson write a prayer list of needs of missionaries and laypersons who minister in difficult places. Covenant with a friend to pray for a specific period of time for these needs.

14. Encourage others to read the book.

Joyce S. Martin, a free-lance writer and assistant editor of the *New England Baptist* who makes her home in Hopkinton, Mass., has visited the Simpsons in the Bronx and has written about the ministry of Sam and Lola and the Wake-Eden and Bronx Baptist churches.

Carol S. Garrett is a homemaker and free-lance writer from Birmingham, Alabama. She holds a degree in journalism from the University of Alabama. Mrs. Garrett is a former public information specialist for Woman's Missionary Union, SBC, where she was employed until 1987. With the birth of her first child in April of that year, she began the challenging career of being a full-time mother. She and her husband, Danny, have a son named Jake. They are active members of Clearview Baptist Church, where Mrs. Garrett serves as church historian and Baptist Women mission study chairman. She is a native of Haleyville, Alabama.

The Church Study Course

The Church Study Course is a Southern Baptist educational system consisting of more than 500 short courses for adults and youth combined with a credit and recognition system. Credit is awarded for each course completed. The credits may be applied to 1 or more of the 25 diplomas.

Complete details about the Church Study Course system, courses available, and diplomas offered may be found in a current copy of the *Church Study Course Catalog* and in the study course section of the *Church Materials Catalog*. The Church Study Course is sponsored by the Sunday School Board, Woman's Missionary Union, and the Brotherhood Commission.

Credit for the course (08139) may be obtained in two ways: (1) Read the book and participate in a 2½-hour study. (2) Read the book and follow the suggestions for individual study in the study section.

Request credit of Form 725, "Church Study Course Enrollment/Credit Request," available from Awards Office, Sunday School Board, 127 Ninth Avenue, North, Nashville, TN 37234.

A record of your awards will be maintained by the Awards Office. Twice each year copies will be sent to churches for distribution to members.